GLUTEN-FREE
AND EASY

GLUTEN-FREE AND EASY

COLLINS & BROWN

The Good Housekeeping website is
www.goodhousekeeping.co.uk

ISBN 978-1-908449-97-9

A catalogue record for this book is available from
the British Library.

Reproduction by Dot Gradations Ltd, UK
Printed and bound by
1010 Printing International Ltd, China

This book can be ordered direct from the publisher.
Contact the marketing department, but try your
bookshop first.

www.anovabooks.com

NOTES

Both metric and imperial measures are given for
the recipes. Follow either set of measures, not a
mixture of both, as they are not interchangeable.

All spoon measures are level.
1 tsp = 5ml spoon; 1 tbsp = 15ml spoon.

Ovens and grills must be preheated to the specified
temperature.

Medium eggs should be used except where
otherwise specified. Free-range eggs are
recommended.

Note that some recipes contain raw or lightly
cooked eggs. The young, elderly, pregnant women
and anyone with an immune-deficiency disease
should avoid these because of the slight risk of
salmonella.

Contents

Start the Day

Essential Know-how

A gluten-free diet is one that excludes the protein gluten. It is the treatment for coeliac disease. This means that your health depends on avoiding gluten in all its various forms and avoiding cross-contamination in the kitchen.

What is coeliac disease?

Coeliac disease is an autoimmune condition, which means the body's immune system attacks its own tissues. In people with coeliac disease this immune reaction is triggered by a protein, gluten. Gluten damages the surface of the intestines and reduces the body's ability to absorb nutrients from food.

What is gluten?

Gluten is a collective name for a type of protein found in three cereals:

❑ Wheat
❑ Barley
❑ Rye

Gluten causes inflammation in the small intestines of people with coeliac disease. Some people react to a similar protein found in oats.

Where is gluten found?

Gluten is found in foods containing the above cereals, including pasta, cakes, breakfast cereals and bread. It can also be found in soups, sauces, sausages, ready meals, cakes, biscuits and puddings (see page 64 – the gluten-free storecupboard).

How can coeliac disease be treated?

There is no cure for coeliac disease, but switching to a gluten-free diet prevents further damage to the lining of your intestines and allows your gut to heal. It helps control the symptoms, such as diarrhoea and stomach pain and also prevents long-term consequences of the disease.

The gluten-free diet

It is important to make sure your gluten-free diet is healthy and balanced. An increase in the range of available gluten-free foods in recent years has made it possible to eat both a healthy and varied gluten-free diet.

Initially, following a gluten-free diet may be frustrating. But with time and patience you'll find that there are many basic foods, such as meat, vegetables, cheese, potatoes, and rice, are naturally gluten-free so you can still include them in your diet. You can also buy gluten-free products, including pasta, pizza bases and bread in supermarkets and health food shops. If you're just starting a gluten-free diet, you should consult a dietitian who can help you identify which foods are safe to eat and which are not. However, if you are unsure, use the lists on page 10 as a general guide.

Being Gluten-free and Easy

Many people think they simply need to cut wheat from their diets — or even just bread — in order to go gluten-free. But it's unfortunately a lot more complicated than that. Gluten appears in many processed foods ranging from sausages to sauces, and it's not always obvious from the ingredients.

Gluten-free foods (safe to eat)

You can eat the following foods which are naturally gluten-free:

- ❏ Most dairy products, such as cheese, butter and milk
- ❏ Eggs
- ❏ Fruit and vegetables
- ❏ Meat, poultry and fish (although not breaded or battered)
- ❏ Potatoes
- ❏ Rice

Make sure that they are not processed or mixed with gluten-containing ingredients. Many cereals and flours can be included in a gluten-free diet including:

- ❏ Gluten-free flours, including rice, corn, soya and potato
- ❏ Arrowroot
- ❏ Buckwheat
- ❏ Corn and cornmeal
- ❏ Millet
- ❏ Sorghum
- ❏ Soya
- ❏ Tapioca

Reading the label

It is important to always check the labels of the foods you buy. Look for the crossed grain symbol on packaging, which means the food is gluten-free. Many foods, particularly those that are processed, contain gluten in additives, such as malt flavouring and modified food starch. If a cereal containing gluten is used as an ingredient it must be listed on the ingredients list. Coeliac UK provides a directory of gluten-free food and drink, which is updated monthly.

What does 'gluten-free' mean?

The term 'gluten-free' implies no gluten, but in practice it is not possible to test for a zero level of gluten. Research has shown that for most people such trace amounts of gluten will not cause any problem. As a result low levels of gluten are allowed in products that are labelled gluten-free. By law, food labelled as 'gluten-free' can contain up to 20 parts per million (ppm) of gluten.

'May contain' gluten

Cross-contamination can occur if gluten-free foods and foods that contain gluten are prepared together or served with the same utensils. It can happen during manufacturing, for example if the same equipment is used to process gluten-containing products. Some food labels include a 'may contain' statement if this is the case. However, you should still check the ingredients list. If you're not sure whether a product contains gluten, don't buy it or check with the manufacturer.

Raspberry and Kiwi Smoothie

Hands-on time: 10 minutes

3 kiwi fruit, peeled and roughly chopped

200g (7oz) fresh or frozen raspberries, thawed if frozen, juices put to one side

200-250ml (7-9fl oz) unsweetened orange juice

4 tbsp Greek yogurt

1 Put the kiwi fruit into a blender. If using fresh raspberries, remove the hulls, then wash and pat the fruit dry with kitchen paper. Add to the blender. If the fruit has been frozen, add the juices as well.

2 Pour in the orange juice and yogurt and blend until smooth, then pour into two glasses and serve.

Serves 2; makes 500–600ml (18fl oz–1 pint)

Summer Berry Smoothie

Hands-on time: 10 minutes

2 large ripe bananas, about 450g (1lb), peeled and chopped

150g (5oz) natural yogurt

500g (1lb 2oz) fresh or frozen summer berries

1 Put the bananas into a blender, add the yogurt and 150ml (¼ pint) water, then whiz until smooth. Add the berries and whiz to a purée.

2 Strain the mixture through a fine nylon sieve into a large jug, using the back of a ladle to press it through the sieve. Pour into six glasses and serve immediately.

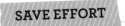

SAVE EFFORT

An easy way to get a brand new dish is to use 6 ripe apricots (or 16 ready-to-eat dried apricots) or 400g (14oz) canned apricots in natural juice instead of the berries.

Serves 6; makes 900ml (1½ pints)

Exotic Fruit Salad

2 oranges

1 mango, peeled, stoned and chopped

450g (1lb) peeled and diced fresh
pineapple

200g (7oz) blueberries

½ Charentais melon, cubed

grated zest and juice of 1 lime

1 Using a sharp knife, peel the oranges, remove the pith and cut the flesh into segments. Put into a bowl.

2 Add the mango, pineapple, blueberries and melon to the bowl, then add the lime zest and juice. Gently mix together and serve immediately.

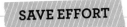

HEALTHY TIP

This dessert is packed with vitamins C and betacarotene (see page 75). Fresh pineapple contains the enzyme bromelain, which aids digestion and is beneficial for inflammatory conditions such as sinusitis and rheumatoid arthritis.

SAVE EFFORT

An easy way to get two brand new dishes is to:

· Use 2 peeled, seeded and chopped papayas instead of the pineapple.

· Mix the seeds of 2 passion fruit with the lime juice before adding to the salad.

Serves 4

Berry Compote

Hands-on time: 15 minutes, plus overnight chilling
Cooking time: 10 minutes, plus cooling

175g (6oz) raspberry conserve

juice of 1 orange

juice of 1 lemon

1 tsp rose water

350g (12oz) strawberries, hulled and
thickly sliced

150g (5oz) blueberries

1 Put the raspberry conserve into a pan with the orange and lemon juices and add 150ml (¼ pint) boiling water. Stir over a low heat to dissolve the conserve, then leave to cool.

2 Stir in the rose water and taste – you may want to add a squeeze more lemon juice if it's too sweet. Put the strawberries and blueberries into a serving bowl and strain the raspberry conserve mixture over them. Cover and chill overnight. Take out of the fridge about 30 minutes before serving.

Serves 4

Apple Compote

Hands-on time: 10 minutes, plus chilling
Cooking time: 5 minutes

250g (9oz) cooking apples, peeled
  and chopped
juice of ½ lemon
1 tbsp golden caster sugar
ground cinnamon to sprinkle

To serve
25g (1oz) raisins
25g (1oz) chopped almonds
1 tbsp natural yogurt

1 Put the apples into a pan with the lemon juice, sugar and 2 tbsp cold water. Cook gently for 5 minutes or until soft. Transfer to a bowl.
2 Sprinkle a little ground cinnamon over the top, then cool and chill. It will keep for up to three days.
3 Serve with the raisins, chopped almonds and yogurt.

SAVE EFFORT

To microwave, put the apples, lemon juice, sugar and water into a microwave-proof bowl, cover loosely with clingfilm and cook on full power in an 850W microwave oven for 4 minutes or until the apples are just soft.

HEALTHY TIP
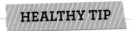

Apples help promote healthy digestion, speeding the passage of waste products through the digestive tract and reducing the risk of constipation. Their high content of pectin also helps lower blood cholesterol levels. Apples are rich in quercetin, a powerful anti-cancer nutrient, as well as immunity-boosting vitamin C.

Serves 2

Apple and Almond Yogurt

Hands-on time: 5 minutes, plus overnight chilling

500g (1lb 2oz) natural yogurt

50g (2oz) flaked almonds

50g (2oz) sultanas

2 apples

1 Put the yogurt into a bowl and add the almonds and sultanas. Grate the apples, add to the bowl and mix together. Chill in the fridge overnight.

2 Use as a topping for breakfast cereal or serve as a snack.

SAVE EFFORT

An easy way to get two brand new dishes is to:
- Use pears instead of apples.
- Replace the sultanas with dried cranberries.

HEALTHY TIP

Natural yogurt contains lactobacillus bacteria, which aids digestion and promotes a healthy immune system. Yogurt is also a good source of protein, B vitamins and bone-strengthening calcium. The almonds add extra calcium while the apples provide useful amounts of fibre and the antioxidant quercetin.

Serves 4

Perfect Scrambled Eggs

There are numerous ways to cook with eggs – from boiling, poaching and scrambling, to making omelettes, soufflés and meringues. Follow these instructions for scrambled eggs with perfect results.

1 Allow 2 eggs per person. Break the eggs into a bowl, then beat well but lightly with a fork and season with salt and ground black pepper.

2 Melt a knob of butter in a small heavy-based pan over a low heat – use a heat diffuser if necessary. (Using a non-stick pan minimises the amount of butter you need to use.)

3 Pour in the eggs and start stirring immediately, using a wooden spoon or a flat-headed spatula to break up the lumps as they form. Keep the eggs moving about as much as possible during cooking.

4 As the eggs start to set, scrape the bottom of the pan to keep the eggs from overcooking and to break up any larger lumps that may form. Your aim is to have a smooth mixture with no noticeable lumps.

5 Scrambled eggs may be well cooked and quite firm, or very 'loose' and runny; this is a matter of taste. They will continue to cook even when taken off the heat, so remove them from the pan when they are still a little softer than you want to serve them.

Microwave scrambled eggs

Put the eggs, milk, if you like, and the butter into a bowl and beat well. Cook on full power (850W) for 1 minute (the mixture should be just starting to set around the edges), then beat again. Cook again on full power for 2–3 minutes, stirring every 30 seconds, until the eggs are cooked the way you like them.

Creamy Baked Eggs

Hands-on time: 5 minutes
Cooking time: about 18 minutes

butter to grease

4 sun-dried tomatoes

4 medium eggs

4 tbsp double cream

salt and freshly ground black pepper

Granary bread to serve (optional)

1 Preheat the oven to 180°C (160°C fan oven) mark 4. Grease four individual ramekins.

2 Put a tomato into each ramekin and season to taste with salt and ground black pepper. Carefully break an egg on top of each tomato, then drizzle 1 tbsp cream over each egg.

3 Bake for 15–18 minutes – the eggs will continue to cook once they have been taken out of the oven.

4 Leave to stand for 2 minutes before serving. Serve with Granary bread, if you like.

Serves 4

Poached Eggs with Mushrooms

TAKE 5

🍴 **Hands-on time:** 15 minutes
Cooking time: about 15 minutes

8 medium-sized flat or portabella
  mushrooms

25g (1oz) butter

8 medium eggs

225g (8oz) baby spinach leaves

4 tsp fresh pesto

HEALTHY TIP

Eggs once had a bad press with
many people believing (wrongly)
that they raised blood cholesterol
levels. However, scientists have
found that most people can safely
eat up to two eggs a day without any
effect on their cholesterol levels.
Eggs are a good source of protein –
two eggs supply roughly one-third
of an adult's daily requirement – as
well as vitamins A and D.

1 Preheat the oven to 200°C (180°C
  fan oven) mark 6. Arrange the
  mushrooms in a single layer in a
  small roasting tin and dot with the
  butter. Roast for 15 minutes or until
  golden brown and soft.

2 Meanwhile, bring a wide shallow
  pan of water to the boil. When the
  mushrooms are half-cooked and the
  water is bubbling furiously, break the
  eggs into the pan, spaced well apart,
  then take the pan off the heat. The eggs
  will take about 6 minutes to cook.

3 When the mushrooms are tender,
  put them on a warmed plate, cover
  and put back into the turned-off oven
  to keep warm.

4 Put the roasting tin over a medium
  heat on the hob and add the spinach.
  Cook, stirring, for about 30 seconds
  until the spinach has just started
  to wilt.

5 The eggs should be set by now, so divide the mushrooms among four warmed plates and top each with a little spinach, a poached egg and a teaspoonful of pesto. For a more substantial meal, serve on 100% rye bread or German pumpernickel.

Serves 4

Perfect Eggs

Follow these tried and tested steps for perfect poached, coddled and boiled eggs.

Perfect poaching

1. Heat about 8cm (3¼in) of lightly salted water in a shallow frying pan to a bare simmer. Crack a very fresh egg into a cup, then slip it into the water. (The whites in a fresh egg are firmer and will form a 'nest' for the yolk, while older egg whites are watery and spread out in the pan.)
2. Cook for 3–4 minutes until the white is barely set. Remove the egg with a slotted spoon and drain on kitchen paper.

Perfect coddling

1. Using a slotted spoon, gently lower the whole eggs into a pan of simmering water, then take the pan off the heat.
2. Leave the eggs to stand in the water for 4–5 minutes, where they will cook gently with the residual heat of the water.

Perfect boiling

Boiling: method 1

1 Bring a small pan of water to the boil. Once the water is boiling, add a medium egg. For a soft-boiled egg, cook for 6 minutes; for a salad egg, cook for 8 minutes; and for a hard-boiled egg, cook for 10 minutes.
2 Remove the egg from the water with a slotted spoon and serve.

Boiling: method 2

1 Put a medium egg into a small pan and cover with cold water. Put on a lid and bring to the boil. When the water begins to boil, take off the lid and cook for 2 minutes for a soft-boiled egg, 5 minutes for a salad egg, and 7 minutes for a hard-boiled egg.
2 Remove the egg from the water with a slotted spoon and serve.

Smoked Haddock Kedgeree

Hands-on time: 10 minutes
Cooking time: 20 minutes

175g (6oz) long-grain rice, washed and drained (see page 94)

450g (1lb) smoked haddock fillets

2 medium eggs, hard-boiled and shelled

75g (3oz) butter

salt and cayenne pepper

freshly chopped parsley to garnish

mixed green salad to serve

1 Cook the rice in a pan of salted fast-boiling water until tender. Drain well and rinse under cold water.

2 Meanwhile, put the haddock into a large frying pan with just enough water to cover. Bring to simmering point, then simmer for 10–15 minutes until tender. Drain, skin and flake the fish, discarding the bones.

3 Chop one egg and slice the other into rings. Melt the butter in a pan, add the cooked rice, fish, chopped egg, salt and cayenne pepper and stir over a medium heat for 5 minutes or until hot. Pile on to a warmed serving dish and garnish with parsley and the sliced egg. Serve with a mixed green salad.

Serves 4

Lunches and Light Bites

Roasted Tomato and Pepper Soup

Hands-on time: 20 minutes
Cooking time: about 1 hour

1.4kg (3lb) full-flavoured tomatoes, preferably vine-ripened

2 red peppers, seeded and chopped

4 garlic cloves, crushed

3 small onions, thinly sliced

20g (¾oz) fresh thyme sprigs

4 tbsp olive oil

4 tbsp Worcestershire sauce

4 tbsp vodka

salt and freshly ground black pepper

6 tbsp double cream to serve

1 Preheat the oven to 200°C (180°C fan oven) mark 6. Put the tomatoes into a large roasting tin with the peppers, garlic and onions. Scatter six of the thyme sprigs over the top, drizzle with oil and roast in the oven for 25 minutes. Turn the vegetables over and roast for a further 30–40 minutes until tender and slightly charred.

2 Put one-third of the vegetables into a blender or food processor with 300ml (½ pint) boiled water. Add the Worcestershire sauce and vodka and season with salt and ground black pepper. Whiz until smooth, then pass through a sieve into a pan.

3 Whiz the remaining vegetables with 450ml (¾ pint) boiled water, then sieve and add to the pan.

4 To serve, warm the soup thoroughly, stirring occasionally. Ladle into warmed bowls, add 1 tbsp double cream to each bowl, then drag a cocktail stick through the cream to swirl. Scatter a few fresh thyme leaves over the top and serve immediately.

Serves 6

Leek and Potato Soup

Hands-on time: 10 minutes
Cooking time: 25 minutes in pan, then 3–4 hours on Low

25g (1oz) butter
1 onion, finely chopped
1 garlic clove, crushed
550g (1¼lb) leeks, trimmed and chopped
200g (7oz) floury potatoes, peeled and sliced
1.2 litres (2 pints) hot vegetable stock
crème fraîche and chopped chives to garnish

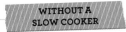

WITHOUT A SLOW COOKER

Complete step 1. In step 2, bring to the boil, then reduce the heat and simmer for 20 minutes or until the potatoes are tender. Complete steps 3 and 4 to finish the recipe.

1 Melt the butter in a pan over a gentle heat. Add the onion and cook for 10–15 minutes until soft. Add the garlic and cook for 1 minute more. Add the leeks and cook for 5–10 minutes until softened. Add the potatoes and toss together with the leeks.

2 Pour in the hot stock and bring to the boil. Transfer the soup to the slow cooker, cover and cook on Low for 3–4 hours until the potatoes are tender.

3 Leave to cool a little, then whiz in batches in a blender or food processor until smooth.

4 Reheat before serving, garnished with crème fraîche and chives.

Serves 4

Split Pea and Ham Soup

Hands-on time: 15 minutes, plus overnight soaking
Cooking time: 15 minutes in pan, then 3–4 hours on High

500g pack dried yellow split peas,
   soaked overnight (see Save Money)

25g (1oz) butter

1 large onion, finely chopped

125g (4oz) rindless smoked streaky
   bacon rashers, roughly chopped

1 garlic clove, crushed

1.7 litres (3 pints) well-flavoured ham or
   vegetable stock

1 bouquet garni (1 bay leaf, a few fresh
   parsley and thyme sprigs)

1 tsp dried oregano

125g (4oz) cooked ham, chopped

salt and freshly ground black pepper

cracked black pepper to serve

1. Drain the soaked split peas. Melt the butter in a large pan, add the onion, bacon and garlic and cook over a low heat for about 10 minutes until the onion is soft.

2. Add the split peas to the pan with the stock. Bring to the boil and use a slotted spoon to remove any scum that comes to the surface. Add the bouquet garni and oregano, then season with salt and ground black pepper. Transfer to the slow cooker, cover and cook on High for 3-4 hours until the peas are very soft.

3. Leave the soup to cool a little, then whiz half the soup in a blender or food processor until smooth. Pour the soup into a pan and reheat, then add the ham and check the seasoning. Ladle into warmed bowls and sprinkle with cracked black pepper to serve.

Dried peas are less expensive than canned ones and they form the base of this comforting soup. First, you need to soak them overnight in about 1 litre (1¾ pints) cold water. If you forget, put them straight into a pan with the water, bring to the boil and cook for 1-2 minutes, then leave to stand for 2 hours before using.

Complete step 1. At the end of step 2, leave the soup in the pan, reduce the heat and simmer, covered, for 45 minutes-1 hour until the peas are very soft. Complete step 3 to finish the recipe.

Serves 6

Full-of-goodness Broth

Hands-on time: 10 minutes
Cooking time: about 8 minutes

1-2 tbsp medium curry paste
(see Healthy Tip)
200ml (7fl oz) reduced-fat coconut milk
600ml (1 pint) hot vegetable stock
200g (7oz) smoked tofu, cubed
2 pak choi, chopped
a handful of sugarsnap peas
4 spring onions, chopped
lime wedges to serve

1 Heat the curry paste in a pan for 1-2 minutes. Add the coconut milk and hot stock and bring to the boil.
2 Add the tofu, pak choi, sugarsnap peas and spring onions, then reduce the heat and simmer for 1-2 minutes.
3 Ladle into warmed bowls and serve each with a wedge of lime to squeeze over the broth.

SAVE EFFORT

An easy way to get a brand new dish is to replace the smoked tofu with shredded leftover roast chicken and simmer for 2-3 minutes.

HEALTHY TIP

Check the ingredients in the curry paste: some may not be suitable for vegetarians.

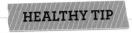

Serves 4

Houmous

400g can chickpeas, drained and rinsed

juice of 1 lemon

4 tbsp tahini

1 garlic clove, crushed

5 tbsp extra virgin olive oil

salt and freshly ground black pepper

pitta bread or toasted flatbreads to serve

1 Put the chickpeas, lemon juice, tahini, garlic and oil into a blender or food processor. Season generously with salt and ground black pepper, then whiz to a paste.

2 Spoon the houmous into a bowl, then cover and chill until needed.

3 Serve with warm pitta bread or toasted flatbreads.

SAVE EFFORT

An easy way to get a brand new dish is to make **Black Olive Houmous**: Stir 25g (1oz) roughly chopped pitted black olives and 1 tsp paprika into the hummus paste. Sprinkle with a little extra paprika and oil, if you like.

Adapting Your Diet

The basics of gluten-free cooking include learning which foods contain gluten and which are safe to eat, how to avoid gluten in processed foods, how to use gluten-free flours, how to convert your favourite recipes to healthy gluten-free recipes and how to eat a nutritionally balanced diet. That's a lot to learn! Here's what you have to avoid.

Always avoid:

- ❑ Wheat
- ❑ Barley
- ❑ Rye
- ❑ Bulgur

Avoid (unless labelled 'gluten-free')
You should check the label before buying any of the following (unless they are labelled as gluten-free or made with corn, rice, soya or other gluten-free grain):

- ❑ Bread
- ❑ Pasta
- ❑ Breakfast cereals
- ❑ Croutons
- ❑ Biscuits and crackers
- ❑ Cakes and pastries
- ❑ Pies

- ❑ Gravies and sauces
- ❑ Salad dressings
- ❑ Soups
- ❑ Processed meats
- ❑ Processed cheese
- ❑ Ready-made pie fillings
- ❑ Condiments and sauces
- ❑ Frozen potatoes with flavoured coatings
- ❑ Flavoured crisps
- ❑ Ready meals
- ❑ Sausages
- ❑ Stock cubes
- ❑ Gravy powders, granules
- ❑ Stuffing
- ❑ Beer – gluten-free beers are now available
- ❑ Gluten in products that are not foods

Gluten may also be found in some non-food products. These include:

- ❑ Lipstick and other cosmetics
- ❑ Postage stamps and gum on envelopes
- ❑ Medication and vitamins that use gluten as a binding agent
- ❑ Food additives, e.g. malt flavouring, modified cornstarch

What to do if you have eaten gluten by mistake

If you accidentally eat a product containing gluten, you may experience abdominal pain and diarrhoea. Some people experience no signs or symptoms after eating gluten but this doesn't mean its damaging their gut. Even trace amounts of gluten in your diet may be damaging whether or not they cause symptoms.

A note on stocks

Gluten-free stock, stock powder and cubes are widely available from supermarkets but check the label says it is gluten-free as some brands contain wheat flour.

Moules Marinière

Hands-on time: 15 minutes
Cooking time: about 20 minutes

2kg (4½lb) fresh mussels, scrubbed, rinsed and beards removed (see Safety Tip)

25g (1oz) butter

4 shallots, finely chopped

2 garlic cloves, crushed

200ml (7fl oz) dry white wine

2 tbsp freshly chopped flat-leafed parsley

100ml (3½fl oz) single cream

salt and freshly ground black pepper

crusty bread to serve

1 Sort the mussels following the Safety Tip opposite. Clean under running water, removing any barnacles or stringy beards with a cutlery knife.

2 Heat the butter in a large non-stick lidded frying pan and sauté the shallots over a medium-high heat for about 10 minutes until soft.

3 Add the garlic, wine and half the parsley to the pan and bring to the boil. Tip in the mussels and reduce the heat a little. Cover and cook for about 5 minutes until all the shells have opened; discard any mussels that remain closed.

4 Lift out the mussels with a slotted spoon and put into serving bowls, then cover with foil to keep warm. Add the cream to the pan, season with salt and ground black pepper and cook for 1–2 minutes to heat through.

5 Pour a little sauce over the mussels and sprinkle with the rest of the parsley. Serve immediately with crusty bread.

Serves 4

Seafood Cocktail

Hands-on time: 15 minutes

½ iceberg lettuce, shredded

175g (6oz) cooked peeled prawns or shrimps, flaked white crab meat or lobster meat, thawed if frozen

cucumber slices, capers or lemon wedges to garnish

For the dressing

2 tbsp mayonnaise

2 tbsp tomato ketchup

2 tbsp natural yogurt

a squeeze of lemon juice, or a dash of Worcestershire sauce

salt and freshly ground black pepper

1 Line four small glasses with the shredded lettuce.

2 To make the dressing, put the mayonnaise into a bowl and mix with the ketchup, yogurt and lemon juice or Worcestershire sauce. Season with salt and ground black pepper to taste.

3 Combine the shellfish and dressing, then pile the mixture into the glasses. Garnish each glass with cucumber slices, capers or lemon wedges and serve immediately.

Serves 4

Courgette and Parmesan Frittata

Hands-on time: 10 minutes
Cooking time: 15 minutes

40g (1½oz) butter

1 small onion, finely sliced

225g (8oz) courgettes, finely sliced

6 medium eggs, beaten

25g (1oz) freshly grated Parmesan, plus shavings to garnish

salt and freshly ground black pepper

crusty bread to serve

SAVE EFFORT

An easy way to get a brand new dish is to use leftover boiled potatoes, cut into small cubes instead of the courgettes.

1 Melt 25g (1oz) of the butter in an 18cm (7in) non-stick frying pan and cook the onion until soft. Add the courgettes and fry gently for 5 minutes or until they begin to soften.

2 Preheat the grill. Add the remaining butter to the frying pan. Season the eggs with salt and ground black pepper and pour into the pan. Cook for 2–3 minutes until golden underneath and cooked around the edges.

3 Scatter the grated cheese over the frittata and put under the preheated grill for 1–2 minutes until just set. Garnish with Parmesan shavings, cut the frittata into quarters and serve with crusty bread.

Serves 4

Aubergine, Feta and Tomato Stacks

Hands-on time: 10 minutes
Cooking time: 12 minutes

200g (7oz) feta, crumbled

2 tbsp olive oil, plus extra to brush

1 garlic clove, crushed, plus 1 garlic clove
to rub

2 plump aubergines, cut into 1cm (½in)
thick slices

a handful of fresh basil leaves, torn

3 large vine-ripened tomatoes, each
sliced into four

salt and freshly ground black pepper

cocktail sticks

rocket and toasted ciabatta to serve

1 Preheat the barbecue or grill. Put the feta into a bowl, stir in the oil and crushed garlic, season with salt and ground black pepper and put to one side.

2 Brush each aubergine slice with a little oil and barbecue or grill for about 6 minutes, turning occasionally, until softened and golden. Take off the heat.

3 Sprinkle a little of the feta mixture on to six of the aubergine slices and put some torn basil leaves on top, then a slice of tomato on each. Season well. Repeat with the feta mixture, basil leaves, aubergine and tomato. Finish with a third aubergine slice and press down firmly.

4 Secure each stack with a cocktail stick. Either use a hinged grill rack, well oiled, or wrap the stacks in foil and barbecue for 2–3 minutes on each side. Serve with rocket and toasted ciabatta rubbed with a garlic clove.

Serves 4

Cheesy Polenta with Tomato Sauce

Hands-on time: 15 minutes
Cooking time: 35 minutes, plus cooling

oil to grease

225g (8oz) polenta

4 tbsp freshly chopped herbs, such as
oregano, chives and flat-leafed parsley

100g (3½oz) freshly grated Parmesan,
plus fresh Parmesan shavings to serve

salt and freshly ground black pepper

For the tomato and basil sauce

1 tbsp vegetable oil

3 garlic cloves, crushed

500g carton creamed tomatoes
or passata

1 bay leaf

1 fresh thyme sprig

caster sugar

3 tbsp freshly chopped basil, plus extra
to serve

1 Lightly oil a 25.5 × 18cm (10 × 7in) dish. Bring 1.1 litres (2 pints) water and ¼ tsp salt to the boil in a large pan. Sprinkle in the polenta, whisking constantly. Reduce the heat and simmer, stirring frequently, for 10–15 minutes until the mixture leaves the sides of the pan.

2 Stir in the herbs and Parmesan and season to taste with salt and ground black pepper. Turn into the prepared dish and leave to cool.

3 Next, make the tomato and basil sauce. Heat the oil in a pan and fry the garlic for 30 seconds (do not brown). Add the creamed tomatoes or passata, the bay leaf, thyme and a large pinch of sugar. Season with salt and ground black pepper and bring to the boil, then reduce the heat and simmer, uncovered, for 5–10 minutes. Remove the bay leaf and thyme sprig and add the chopped basil.

4 To serve, cut the polenta into pieces and lightly brush with oil. Preheat a griddle and fry for 3-4 minutes on each side, or grill under a preheated grill for 7-8 minutes on each side. Serve with the tomato and basil sauce, fresh Parmesan shavings and chopped basil.

SAVE TIME

To prepare ahead, complete the recipe to the end of step 3. Cover and chill separately for up to two days. Complete the recipe to serve.

Serves 6

Broad Bean and Feta Salad

Hands-on time: 10 minutes
Cooking time: 5 minutes

225g (8oz) podded broad beans
   (see Save Effort)
100g (3½oz) feta, chopped
2 tbsp freshly chopped mint
2 tbsp extra virgin olive oil
a squeeze of lemon juice
salt and freshly ground black pepper
lemon wedges to serve (optional)

1 Cook the beans in salted boiling water
  for 3–5 minutes until tender. Drain,
  then plunge them into cold water and
  drain again. Remove their skins, if you
  like (see Save Effort).

2 Tip the beans into a bowl and add the
  feta, mint, oil and a squeeze of lemon
  juice. Season well with salt and ground
  black pepper and toss together. Serve
  with lemon wedges, if you like.

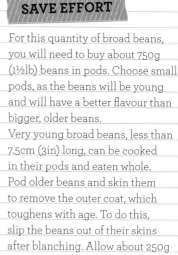

SAVE EFFORT

For this quantity of broad beans,
you will need to buy about 750g
(1½lb) beans in pods. Choose small
pods, as the beans will be young
and will have a better flavour than
bigger, older beans.

Very young broad beans, less than
7.5cm (3in) long, can be cooked
in their pods and eaten whole.
Pod older beans and skin them
to remove the outer coat, which
toughens with age. To do this,
slip the beans out of their skins
after blanching. Allow about 250g
(9oz) weight of whole beans in pods
per person.

Serves 2

Smoked Mackerel Citrus Salad

Hands-on time: 10 minutes
Cooking time: 5 minutes

200g (7oz) green beans

200g (7oz) smoked mackerel fillets

125g (4oz) mixed watercress, spinach
and rocket

4 spring onions, sliced

1 avocado, halved, stoned, peeled
and sliced

For the dressing

1 tbsp olive oil

1 tbsp freshly chopped coriander

grated zest and juice of 1 orange

1 Preheat the grill. Blanch the green beans in boiling water for 3 minutes or until they are just tender. Drain and rinse under cold running water, then drain well again and tip into a bowl.

2 Cook the mackerel under the hot grill for 2 minutes or until warmed through. Flake into bite-size pieces, discard the skin and add the fish to the bowl with the salad leaves, spring onions and avocado.

3 Whisk all the dressing ingredients together in a small bowl. Pour over the salad, toss well and serve immediately.

SAVE MONEY

Leftover mackerel fillets can be turned into a quick pâté. Whiz in a food processor with the zest of a lemon and enough crème fraîche to make a spreadable consistency.

Serves 6

Midweek Suppers

The Gluten-free Storecupboard

Here's a quick guide to stocking your storecupboard with gluten-free foods. It will help you decide which foods you can eat and which you should avoid. There are some foods that you will need to check in the middle column – it is always safest to check the packaging.

	Gluten-free food	Foods to check	Gluten containing foods
CEREALS & FLOUR	Corn, cornflour, rice, rice flour, arrowroot, amaranth, buckwheat, millet, quinoa, sorghum, soya flour, potato starch, potato flour, gram flour, polenta (cornmeal), sago, tapioca, cassava, urid flour	Flavoured savoury rice products, oats	Wheat, bulgur wheat, durum wheat, wheat bran, wheat rusk, wheat flour, semolina, couscous, barley malt, barley flour, rye, rye flour, triticale, kamut, spelt, baking powder
BREAKFAST CEREALS, BREADS, CAKES & BISCUITS	Gluten-free breads, biscuits, crackers, cakes, pizza bases, rolls & flour mixes. Gluten-free muesli, cereals, buckwheat flakes	Meringues, macaroons Porridge oats	All breads, chapattis, biscuits, crackers, cakes, pastries, scones, muffins, pizza made from wheat, rye or barley flour. Wheat-based breakfast cereals, muesli
PASTA & NOODLES	Corn pasta, rice pasta, gluten-free pasta, rice noodles		Canned, dried & fresh wheat noodles and pasta
FRUIT & VEGETABLES	All fresh, frozen, canned & dried fruits and vegetables	Fruit pie fillings, oven, microwave & frozen chips, instant mash, waffles	Fruit pie fillings

	Gluten-free food	Foods to check	Gluten containing foods
DAIRY PRODUCTS & EGGS	All cheeses, all milk (liquid & dried), all cream (single, double, whipping, clotted, soured & crème fraîche), buttermilk, natural yogurt, plain fromage frais Eggs	Coffee & tea whiteners, oat milk, fruit & flavoured yogurt/fromage frais, soya desserts	Yoghurt & fromage frais containing muesli or cereals
MEAT & POULTRY	All fresh meats & poultry, smoked meats, cured pure meats, plain cooked meats	Meat pastes, pates, sausages, burgers	Meat & poultry cooked in batter or breadcrumbs, faggots, rissoles, haggis, breaded ham, Scotch eggs
FISH & SHELLFISH	All fresh fish & shellfish, smoked, kippered & dried fish, fish canned in oil or brine	Fish in sauce, fish pastes & pâtés	Fish in batter or breadcrumbs, fish cakes, taramasalata, fish fingers
FATS & OILS	Butter, margarine, lard, cooking oils, ghee, reduced & low-fat spreads	Suet	
SNACKS	Homemade popcorn, rice cakes, rice crackers, gluten-free crackers & pretzels. All plain nuts & seeds	Dry roasted nuts	Snacks made from wheat, rye, barley, pretzels
DRINKS	Tea, coffee, cocoa, fruit juice, squash, clear fizzy drinks, wine, spirits, cider, sherry, port, liqueurs, gluten-free beers	Drinking chocolate, cloudy fizzy drinks, vending machine hot chocolate	Malted milk drinks, barely waters/squash, beer, lager, ales, stouts
DESSERTS	Rice pudding, jellies, sorbet		Puddings, pastry & pancakes made from wheat flour
SUGARS	Sugar, honey, plain chocolate	Confectionery, chocolate bars	
SAUCES & CONDIMENTS	Salt, pepper, spices	Stock cubes, spice mixes	Gravy, bottles & packet sauces, stuffing

Mushroom and Bean Hotpot

Slow Cooker Recipe

Hands-on time: 15 minutes
Cooking time: 15 minutes in pan, then 2–3 hours on Low

3 tbsp olive oil

700g (1½lb) chestnut mushrooms, roughly chopped

1 large onion, finely chopped

2 tbsp gluten-free plain flour

2 tbsp mild curry paste

150ml (¼ pint) dry white wine

400g can chopped tomatoes

2 tbsp sun-dried tomato paste

2 × 400g cans mixed beans, drained and rinsed

3 tbsp mango chutney

3 tbsp freshly chopped coriander and mint

1 Heat the oil in a large pan over a low heat. Add the mushrooms and onion and fry until the onion is soft and dark golden. Stir in the flour and curry paste and cook for 1–2 minutes, then add the wine, tomatoes, tomato paste and beans.

2 Bring to the boil, then transfer to the slow cooker. Cover and cook on Low for 2–3 hours.

3 Stir in the mango chutney and herbs and serve.

WITHOUT A SLOW COOKER

Complete step 1. At the start of step 2, leave the mixture in the pan, bring to the boil, then reduce the heat and simmer for 30 minutes or until most of the liquid has reduced. Complete step 3 to finish the recipe.

Serves 6

Perfect Flavourings

Many stir-fry and curry recipes begin by cooking garlic, ginger and spring onions as the basic flavourings. Spicier dishes may include chillies, lemongrass or a prepared spice paste such as Thai curry paste.

Ginger

Grating

1. Cut off a piece of the root and peel with a vegetable peeler. Cut off any brown spots.
2. Rest the grater on a board or small plate and grate the ginger. Discard any large fibres adhering to the pulp.

Pressing

1. If you just need the ginger juice, cut off a piece of the root and peel with a vegetable peeler. Cut off any brown spots.
2. Cut the ginger into small chunks, put into a garlic press and squeeze over a small bowl to extract the juice.

Slicing, shredding and chopping

1. Cut off a piece of the root and peel with a vegetable peeler. Cut off any brown spots.
2. Stack the slices and cut into shreds.
3. To chop, stack the shreds and cut across into small pieces.

Garlic

1. Put the clove on a chopping board and place the flat side of a large knife on top of it. Press down firmly on the flat of the blade to crush the clove and break the papery skin.
2. Cut off the base of the clove and slip the garlic out of its skin. It should come away easily.

Crushing

1 After step 2 on the previous page, the whole clove can be put into a garlic press.
2 To crush with a knife: roughly chop the peeled cloves with a pinch of salt. Press down hard with the edge of a large knife tip (with the blade facing away from you), then drag the blade along the garlic while still pressing hard. Continue to do this, dragging the knife tip over the garlic.

2

Slicing

Using a rocking motion with the knife tip on the board, slice the garlic as thinly as you need.

Shredding and chopping

Holding the slices together, shred them across the slices. Chop the shreds if you need chopped garlic.

Spring onions

Cut off the roots and trim any coarse or withered green parts. Slice diagonally, or shred by cutting into 5cm (2in) lengths, then slicing down the lengths, or chop finely, according to the recipe.

Chillies

1 Cut off the cap and slit the chilli open lengthways. Using a spoon, scrape out the seeds and the pith.
2 For diced chilli, cut into thin shreds lengthways, then cut crossways.

SAFETY TIP

· Chillies vary enormously in strength, from quite mild to blisteringly hot, depending on the type of chilli and its ripeness. Taste a small piece first to check it's not too hot for you.
· Be extremely careful when handling chillies not to touch or rub your eyes with your fingers, as they will sting. Wash knives immediately after handling chillies for the same reason. As a precaution, use rubber gloves when preparing them, if you like.

Veggie Curry

Hands-on time: 5 minutes
Cooking time: 12 minutes

1 tbsp medium curry paste

227g can chopped tomatoes

150ml (¼ pint) hot vegetable stock

200g (7oz) vegetables, such as broccoli, courgettes and sugarsnap peas, roughly chopped

½ × 400g can chickpeas, drained and rinsed

griddled wholemeal pitta bread and natural yogurt to serve

1 Heat the curry paste in a large heavy-based pan for 1 minute, stirring the paste to warm the spices. Add the tomatoes and hot stock and bring to the boil, then reduce the heat to a simmer and add the vegetables. Simmer for 5–6 minutes until the vegetables are tender.

2 Stir in the chickpeas and heat for 1–2 minutes until hot. Serve the vegetable curry with a griddled wholemeal pitta and some yogurt.

Serves 1

Oven-poached Cod with Herbs

Hands-on time: 10 minutes
Cooking time: 10 minutes

10 spring onions, sliced
2 garlic cloves, crushed
6 tbsp shredded fresh mint
6 tbsp freshly chopped flat-leafed
   parsley
juice of ½ lemon
150ml (¼ pint) fish, chicken or
   vegetable stock
4 cod fillets, about 200g (7oz) each
salt and freshly ground black pepper
lemon wedges to garnish
mashed potatoes to serve

1 Preheat the oven to 230°C (210°C fan oven) mark 8. Combine the spring onions (putting some of the green part to one side), garlic, mint, parsley, lemon juice and stock in an ovenproof dish that can hold the cod in a single layer.

2 Put the cod on the herb and garlic mixture and turn to moisten. Season with salt and ground black pepper, then roast for 8–10 minutes.

3 Take out of the oven, sprinkle with the reserved spring onion, garnish with lemon wedges and serve with mashed potatoes.

SAVE EFFORT

An easy way to get a brand new dish is to use sea bass, gurnard or pollack instead of cod.

The flat-leafed parsley used in this dish is rich in vitamin C (weight for weight it contains three times as much vitamin C as oranges), betacarotene (an antioxidant that helps combat harmful free radicals and promotes healthy skin), folate and iron. It contains flavanoids and other phytochemicals, recognised as having cancer-fighting properties. Mint is also a source of anti-cancer substances and well-recognised for soothing the digestive tract.

Serves 4

Crispy Crab Cakes

Hands-on time: 20 minutes
Cooking time: about 8 minutes

250g (9oz) white crab meat

4 spring onions, thinly sliced

7.5cm (3in) piece fresh root ginger,
    peeled and grated

4 tbsp finely chopped chives

1 fresh red chilli, seeded and finely
    chopped (see Safety Tip, page 71)

2 large eggs

200g (7oz) fresh white gluten-free
    breadcrumbs

3 tbsp vegetable oil

4 tbsp mayonnaise

finely grated zest and juice of ½ lime,
    plus lime wedges to serve

salt and freshly ground black pepper

crisp green salad to serve

1 Mix the crab, spring onions, ginger, chives, chilli, eggs and breadcrumbs together in a large bowl. Season with salt and ground black pepper and form into 16 round patties.

2 Heat the oil in a large non-stick frying pan and fry the crab cakes for 6 minutes, turning once, until golden and crisp (cook in batches, if necessary).

3 Meanwhile, mix the mayonnaise, lime zest and juice together in a bowl. Season well with salt and ground black pepper and serve with the crab cakes, lime wedges and a crisp green salad.

Serves 4

Moroccan Chicken Casserole

Hands-on time: 20 minutes, plus marinating (optional)
Cooking time: about 45 minutes

2 garlic cloves

½ tsp smoked paprika

¼ tsp ground turmeric

1 tsp cumin seeds

2 tbsp olive oil

8 skinless chicken thighs

2 onions, thinly sliced

½ lemon, cut into thin rounds
  (pips removed)

1 tbsp cornflour

400g can lentils, drained and rinsed

a large handful of fresh coriander,
  chopped

salt and freshly ground black pepper

boiled wild rice to serve

1 Pound together the garlic, paprika, turmeric, cumin and seasoning to taste in a pestle and mortar. Mix in 1 tbsp of the oil to make a paste, then scrape the paste into a bowl and add the chicken thighs. Rub the marinade over the chicken, cover with clingfilm and leave to chill for 1 hour, if you have time.

2 Heat the remaining oil in a large pan and gently cook the onions for 10 minutes or until softened. Add the chicken (scraping in any marinade left behind in the bowl) and lemon slices and fry to brown them.

3 Stir in the cornflour, mix well, then add enough water to come halfway up the chicken. Bring to the boil. Cover the pan with a lid, then reduce the heat and simmer for 25 minutes, stirring occasionally, until the chicken is cooked through.

4 Stir in the lentils and most of the coriander and heat through. Check the seasoning, garnish with the remaining coriander and serve with wild rice.

Serves 4

Spanish Chicken

Slow Cooker Recipe

Hands-on time: 15 minutes, plus infusing
Cooking time: about 20 minutes in pan, then 1–2 hours on Low

1.1 litres (2 pints) chicken stock

1 tsp ground turmeric

2 tbsp vegetable oil

4 boneless, skinless chicken thighs, roughly diced

1 onion, chopped

1 red pepper, seeded and sliced

50g (2oz) chorizo sausage, diced

2 garlic cloves, crushed

300g (11oz) long-grain rice, washed and drained (see page 94)

125g (4oz) frozen peas

salt and freshly ground black pepper

3 tbsp freshly chopped flat-leafed parsley to garnish

crusty bread to serve

1 Heat the stock, add the turmeric and leave for at least 5 minutes. Heat the oil in a frying pan and fry the chicken for 10 minutes or until golden. Transfer to the slow cooker.

2 Add the onion to the pan and cook for until soft. Add the red pepper and chorizo and cook for 5 minutes, then add the garlic and cook for 1 minute.

3 Add the rice and mix. Pour in the stock and peas and season. Transfer to the slow cooker and stir. Cover and cook on Low for 1–2 hours until the rice is tender and the chicken is cooked. Check the seasoning. Garnish with parsley and serve with bread.

Complete step 1, putting the chicken on a plate. At the end of step 2, put the chicken back into the pan, add the rice and one-third of the stock, then mix and simmer until the liquid has been absorbed. Add the rest of the stock with the peas, and bring to the boil. Reduce the heat to low and cook for 15–20 minutes until no liquid remains. Garnish and serve as described in step 4.

Serves 4

Simple Paella

Hands-on time: 15 minutes, plus infusing
Cooking time: 50 minutes

1 litre (1¾ pints) chicken stock
½ tsp saffron threads
5 tbsp extra virgin olive oil
6 boneless, skinless chicken thighs,
    each cut into three pieces
1 large onion, chopped
4 large garlic cloves, crushed
1 tsp paprika
2 red peppers, seeded and sliced
400g can chopped tomatoes
350g (12oz) long-grain rice
200ml (7fl oz) dry sherry
500g (1lb 2oz) cooked mussels
    (see Save Time)
200g (7oz) cooked and peeled tiger prawns
juice of ½ lemon
salt and freshly ground black pepper
fresh flat-leafed parsley to garnish
lemon wedges to serve

1 Heat the stock, then add the saffron and leave to infuse for 30 minutes.

2 Heat half the oil in a frying pan and fry the chicken in batches for 3–5 minutes until golden brown. Put the chicken to one side. Reduce the heat slightly. Add the remaining oil and fry the onion for 5 minutes or until soft. Add the garlic and paprika and stir for 1 minute. Add the chicken, red peppers and tomatoes and stir in the rice. Add one-third of the stock and bring to the boil, then season with salt and ground black pepper. Reduce the heat to a simmer and cook, uncovered, stirring constantly until most of the liquid has been absorbed.

3 Heat the remaining stock and add a little at a time, letting the rice absorb it before adding more – this should take about 25 minutes. Add the sherry and cook for 2 minutes – the rice should be quite wet, as it will continue to absorb liquid. Stir in the mussels and prawns, with their juices, and the

lemon juice and cook for 5 minutes to heat through. Adjust the seasoning. Garnish with the parsley and serve with lemon wedges.

SAVE TIME

Ready-cooked mussels are available vacuum-packed from supermarkets. Alternatively, cook fresh mussels (see pages 48–49).

Serves 6

Pan-fried Chorizo and Potato

Hands-on time: 10 minutes
Cooking time: 30 minutes

2 tbsp olive oil

450g (1lb) potatoes, cut into
   2.5cm (1in) cubes

2 red onions, sliced

1 red pepper, seeded and chopped

1 tsp paprika

300g (11oz) piece of chorizo sausage,
   skinned and cut into chunky slices

250g (9oz) cherry tomatoes

100ml (3½fl oz) dry sherry

2 tbsp freshly chopped flat-leafed parsley

1 Heat the oil in a large heavy-based frying pan over a medium heat. Add the potato cubes and fry for 7–10 minutes until lightly browned, turning regularly.

2 Reduce the heat, add the onions and red pepper and continue to cook for 10 minutes, stirring from time to time, until they have softened but not browned.

3 Add the paprika and chorizo and cook for 5 minutes, stirring from time to time.

4 Add the tomatoes and pour in the sherry. Stir everything together and cook for 5 minutes or until the sherry has reduced and the tomatoes have softened and warmed through.

5 Sprinkle the chopped parsley over the top and serve.

Serves 4

One-pot Spicy Beef

Hands-on time: 10 minutes
Cooking time: 40 minutes

2 tsp sunflower oil

1 large onion, roughly chopped

1 garlic clove, finely chopped

1 small fresh red chilli, seeded and finely chopped (see Safety Tip, page 71)

2 red peppers, seeded and roughly chopped

2 celery sticks, diced

400g (14oz) lean beef mince

400g can chopped tomatoes

2 × 400g cans mixed beans, drained and rinsed

1–2 tsp Tabasco

2–3 tbsp roughly chopped fresh coriander to garnish (optional)

salsa (see Save Time) and soft flour tortillas or boiled basmati rice to serve

1 Heat the oil in a large heavy-based frying pan over a medium heat. Add the onion to the pan with 2 tbsp water and cook for 10 minutes or until soft. Add the garlic and chilli and cook for a further 1–2 minutes until golden. Add the red peppers and celery and cook for 5 minutes.

2 Add the beef to the pan and brown it all over. Add the tomatoes, beans and Tabasco, then simmer for 20 minutes.

3 Garnish with coriander, if you like, and serve with salsa and tortillas or basmati rice.

SAVE TIME

To make a quick salsa, peel and roughly chop ½ ripe avocado. Put into a bowl with 4 roughly chopped tomatoes, 1 tsp olive oil and the juice of ½ lime. Mix well.

Serves 4

Chilli Steak and Corn on the Cob

Hands-on time: 5 minutes, plus chilling
Cooking time: 20 minutes

50g (2oz) butter, softened

1 large fresh red chilli, seeded and finely chopped (see Safety Tip, page 71)

1 garlic clove, crushed

25g (1oz) freshly grated Parmesan

1 tbsp finely chopped fresh basil

4 corn on the cob, each cut into three pieces

1 tbsp olive oil

4 sirloin steaks, about 150g (5oz) each

mixed green salad to serve

1 Put the butter into a bowl and beat with a wooden spoon. Add the chilli, garlic, Parmesan and basil and mix everything together. Cover and chill to firm up.

2 Meanwhile, bring a large pan of water to the boil. Add the corn, cover to bring back to the boil, then reduce the heat and simmer, half-covered, for about 10 minutes until tender. Drain well.

3 Heat the oil in a large frying pan or griddle over a medium heat. Cook the steaks for 2–3 minutes on each side for medium-rare, or 3–4 minutes for medium.

4 Divide the corn and steaks among four warmed plates and top with the chilled butter. Serve immediately, with a mixed green salad.

Turkish Lamb Stew

Hands-on time: 10 minutes
Cooking time: about 2 hours

2 tbsp olive oil

400g (14oz) lean lamb fillet, cubed

1 red onion, sliced

1 garlic clove, crushed

1 potato, quartered

400g can chopped plum tomatoes

1 red pepper, seeded and sliced

200g (7oz) canned chickpeas, drained
and rinsed

1 aubergine, cut into chunks

200ml (7fl oz) lamb stock

1 tbsp red wine vinegar

1 tsp each freshly chopped thyme,
rosemary and oregano

8 black olives, halved and pitted

salt and freshly ground black pepper

1 Heat 1 tbsp of the oil in a large
flameproof casserole and brown the
lamb over a high heat. Reduce the
heat and add the remaining oil, the
onion and garlic and cook until soft.

2 Preheat the oven to 170°C (150°C
fan oven) mark 3. Add the potato,
tomatoes, red pepper, chickpeas,
aubergine, stock, vinegar and herbs
to the pan. Season to taste, then stir
and bring to the boil. Cover the pan,
transfer to the oven and cook for
1–1½ hours until the lamb is tender.

3 About 15 minutes before the end of
the cooking time, add the olives.

Serves 4

Cooking for Friends

Perfect Rice

There are two main types of rice: long-grain and short-grain. Long-grain rice is generally served as an accompaniment, such as basmati rice in Indian cooking; the most commonly used type of long-grain rice in Southeast Asian cooking is jasmine rice, also known as Thai fragrant rice. It has a distinctive taste and slightly sticky texture. There are various types of short-grain rice, including that used to make sushi. If you cook rice often, you may want to invest in a rice steamer. They are available from Asian supermarkets and some kitchen shops and give good, consistent results.

Thai rice

To serve six, you will need:
500g (1lb 2oz) Thai rice, a handful of fresh mint leaves, salt.

1 Cook the rice and mint in lightly salted boiling water for 10–12 minutes until tender. Drain well and serve.

Basmati rice

Put the rice into a bowl and cover with cold water. Stir until this becomes cloudy, then drain and repeat until the water is clear. Soak the rice for 30 minutes, then drain before cooking.

Long-grain rice

Long-grain rice needs no special preparation, although it should be washed to remove excess starch. Put the rice in a bowl and cover with cold water. Stir until this becomes cloudy, then drain and repeat until the water is clear.

1   Use 50–75g (2–3oz) raw rice per person; measured by volume 50–75ml (2–2½fl oz). Measure the rice by volume and put it into a pan with a pinch of salt and twice the volume of boiling water (or stock).

2   Bring to the boil. Reduce the heat to low and set the timer for the time stated on the pack. The rice should be al dente: tender with a bite at the centre.

3   When the rice is cooked, fluff up the grains with a fork.

Saffron rice

To serve eight, you will need:
500g (1lb 2oz) basmati rice, 900ml
(1½ pints) stock made with 1½
chicken stock cubes, 5 tbsp sunflower
or light vegetable oil, ½ tsp saffron
threads, salt, 75g (3oz) blanched
and coarsely chopped almonds and
pistachio nuts, to garnish (optional).

1 Put the rice into a bowl and cover
   with warm water, then drain well
   through a sieve.
2 Put the stock, oil and a good pinch
   of salt into a pan, then cover and
   bring to the boil. Add the saffron
   and the rice.
3 Cover the pan and bring the stock
   back to the boil, then stir, reduce
   the heat to low, replace the lid and
   cook gently for 10 minutes or until
   little holes appear all over the
   surface of the cooked rice and the
   grains are tender. Leave to stand,
   covered, for 15 minutes.
4 Fluff up the rice with a fork and
   transfer it to a warmed serving
   dish. Sprinkle the nuts on top of
   the rice, if you like, and serve.

Basic risotto

Italian risotto is made with medium-
grain Arborio, vialone nano or
carnaroli rice, which release starch
to give a rich, creamy texture. It is
traditionally cooked on the hob, but
can also be cooked in the oven by
adding all the liquid in one go and
cooking until the liquid is absorbed.

To serve four, you will need:
1 chopped onion, 50g (2oz) butter,
900ml (1½ pints) chicken stock, 225g
(8oz) risotto rice, 50g (2oz) freshly
grated Parmesan, plus extra to serve.

1   Gently fry the onion in the butter for 10–15 minutes until very lightly coloured. Heat the stock in a separate pan and keep at a simmer. Add the rice to the butter and onion and stir for 1–2 minutes until well coated.

2   Add a ladleful of hot stock and stir constantly until absorbed. Add the remaining stock a ladleful at a time, stirring, until the rice is al dente (tender but still with bite at the centre) – 20–30 minutes (you may not need all the stock). Stir in the Parmesan and serve immediately with extra cheese.

Curried Coconut and Vegetable Rice

Hands-on time: 15 minutes
Cooking time: about 35 minutes, plus standing

1 large aubergine, about 300g (11oz)

1 large butternut squash, about 500g (1lb 2oz), peeled and seeded

250g (9oz) dwarf green beans, trimmed

100ml (3½fl oz) vegetable oil

1 large onion, chopped

1 tbsp black mustard seeds

3 tbsp korma paste

350g (12oz) basmati rice, washed (see page 94)

400ml can coconut milk

200g (7oz) baby spinach leaves

salt and freshly ground black pepper

1 Cut the aubergine and butternut squash into 2cm (¾in) cubes. Slice the green beans into 2cm (¾in) pieces.

2 Heat the oil in a large pan. Add the onion and cook for about 5 minutes until a light golden colour. Add the mustard seeds and cook, stirring, until they begin to pop. Stir in the korma paste and cook for 1 minute.

3 Add the aubergine and cook, stirring, for 5 minutes. Add the butternut squash, beans, rice and 2 tsp salt and mix well. Pour in the coconut milk and add 600ml (1 pint) water. Bring to the boil, then reduce the heat, cover the pan and simmer for 15–18 minutes.

4 When the rice and vegetables are cooked, remove the lid and put the spinach leaves on top. Cover and leave, off the heat, for 5 minutes. Gently stir the wilted spinach through the rice, check the seasoning and serve immediately.

Serves 6

Vegetable Moussaka

Hands-on time: 15 minutes
Cooking time: about 1½ hours

450g (1lb) potatoes, peeled and cut lengthways into 5mm (¼in) slices

1 aubergine, sliced into rounds

1 large red onion, cut into wedges

2 red peppers, seeded and sliced

4 tbsp olive oil

2 tbsp freshly chopped thyme

225g (8oz) tomatoes, thickly sliced

2 garlic cloves, sliced

250g (9oz) passata

250g (9oz) soft goat's cheese (see Healthy Tip)

300g (11oz) natural yogurt

3 medium eggs

25g (1oz) Parmesan, grated (see as above)

salt and freshly ground black pepper

green salad to serve

1 Preheat the oven to 230°C (210°C fan oven) mark 8. Boil the potatoes in a pan of lightly salted water for 5 minutes. Drain and put into a large roasting tin with the aubergine, onion and red peppers. Drizzle with the oil, add the thyme, toss and season with salt and ground black pepper. Roast for 30 minutes, stirring occasionally.

2 Add the tomatoes and garlic and roast for 15 minutes, then take out of the oven. Reduce the oven temperature to 200°C (180°C fan oven) mark 6.

3 Put half the vegetables into a 1.7 litre (3 pint) ovenproof dish, then spoon half the passata over them and spread the goat's cheese on top. Repeat with the rest of the vegetables and passata. Mix together the yogurt, eggs and Parmesan and season, then pour over the top. Cook in the oven for 45 minutes or until heated through. Serve with a green salad.

HEALTHY TIP

If making this for vegetarians, most supermarkets and cheese shops now stock an excellent range of vegetarian cheeses, produced using vegetarian rennet.

SAVE EFFORT

An easy way to get a brand new dish is to use sliced sweet potatoes, or butternut squash, seeded and cut into chunks, instead of the potatoes.

Serves 6

Spanish Fish Stew

Hands-on time: 10 minutes
Cooking time: 1 hour 10 minutes

350g (12oz) small salad potatoes, halved

175g (6oz) chorizo sausage, skinned and roughly chopped

350g jar roasted peppers in olive oil, drained and chopped, oil put to one side

1 garlic clove, crushed

2 small red onions, cut into thick wedges

175ml (6fl oz) dry white wine

300g (11oz) passata

25g (1oz) pitted black olives

450g (1lb) chunky white fish, such as cod and haddock, cut into large cubes

salt and freshly ground black pepper

freshly chopped flat-leafed parsley to garnish

1 Preheat the oven to 170°C (150°C fan oven) mark 3. Put the potatoes, chorizo, roasted peppers, garlic, onions, wine and passata into a large flameproof casserole with 2 tbsp of the oil from the peppers. Season with salt and ground black pepper.

2 Bring to the boil over a medium heat, then cover with a tight-fitting lid and cook in the oven for 45 minutes.

3 Add the olives and fish and put back in the oven for 15 minutes or until the fish is opaque and completely cooked through. Spoon into warmed bowls and serve garnished with chopped parsley.

SAVE TIME

Passata is a useful ingredient to have in your storecupboard. It is made from ripe tomatoes that have been puréed and sieved to make a very smooth sauce, and can be used in sauces and stews.

Serves 4

Chinese-style Fish

Hands-on time: 10 minutes
Cooking time: 10 minutes

2 tsp sunflower oil

1 small onion, finely chopped

1 fresh green chilli, seeded and finely
   chopped (see Safety Tip, page 71)

2 courgettes, thinly sliced

125g (4oz) frozen peas (thawed)

350g (12oz) skinless haddock fillet, cut
   into bite-size pieces

2 tsp lemon juice

4 tbsp hoisin sauce

lime wedges to serve

1 Heat the oil in a large non-stick frying
   pan. Add the onion, chilli, courgettes
   and peas and stir over a high heat
   for 5 minutes or until the onion and
   courgettes begin to soften.

2 Add the fish to the pan with the lemon
   juice, hoisin sauce and 150ml (¼ pint)
   water. Bring to the boil, then reduce
   the heat and simmer, uncovered, for
   2–3 minutes until the fish is cooked
   through. Serve with lime wedges to
   squeeze over.

SAVE EFFORT

An easy way to get a brand new
dish is to use sea bass, sea bream or
gurnard instead of the haddock.

Serves 4

Top 5 Tips for Successful Gluten-free Eating

Focus on fresh produce

Focus on cooking with naturally gluten-free foods like unprocessed fresh fruits, vegetables, eggs, meats, fish and poultry and gluten-free cooking becomes easier and healthier.

Eat as simply as you can, using only fresh herbs, salt and ground black pepper to season your foods. Try grains such as corn in moderation, and don't introduce packaged foods until you have a better feel for the diet and how it affects your system.

Scrutinise the menu

Gluten-free restaurant dining can be tricky — many chefs aren't very familiar with the gluten-free diet, and mistakes are pretty common. Call ahead and speak to the chef or waiter – highlight which foods are gluten-free and provide specific examples of what is not safe (e.g. wheat flour in sauces, breadcrumbs, croutons). If there is nothing suitable on the menu, ask if the chef could cook something else gluten-free. Many restaurant chefs are happy to do this once they know the reason for the request.

Check the label for oats

Oats do not contain gluten, but many people with coeliac disease avoid eating them because they can become contaminated with other cereals that do contain gluten during growing and processing. For this reason, doctors and dietitians usually recommend avoiding oats unless they are specifically labelled gluten-free.

Get enough fibre

To ensure you are getting enough fibre and B-vitamins, eat a wide variety of gluten-free grains, fruit and vegetables. Grains such as corn, soya, potato, quinoa, millet, arrowroot, buckwheat, amaranth and rice flours can increase the nutrient profile of the gluten-free diet. Opt for whole grain gluten-free flour mixes which contain more fibre than the highly refined tapioca, white rice and corn starch flours.

Know your drinks

- ❑ Cider, wine, sherry, spirits, port and liqueurs are suitable for people with coeliac disease
- ❑ Beer, lagers, stouts and ales contain varying amounts of gluten and are therefore not safe for people with coeliac disease. You can buy gluten-free beers and lagers and these are usually found in 'Free From' section of the supermarket and some health food stores
- ❑ Fruit juice, flavoured waters, cordials and fizzy drinks are gluten-free. Barley squashes are not suitable

Chicken Cacciatore

Hands-on time: 5 minutes
Cooking time: 40 minutes

2 tbsp olive oil

8 boneless, skinless chicken thighs

2 garlic cloves, crushed

1 tsp dried thyme

1 tsp dried tarragon

150ml (¼ pint) white wine

400g can chopped tomatoes

12 pitted black olives

12 capers, rinsed and drained

freshly ground black pepper

boiled brown rice and broad beans or
  peas to serve

SAVE EFFORT

As an alternative, shred the chicken once cooked and put back into the tomato mixture to make a hearty pasta sauce.

1 Heat the oil in a flameproof casserole over a high heat. Add the chicken and brown all over. Reduce the heat and add the garlic, thyme, tarragon and wine to the casserole. Stir for 1 minute, then add the tomatoes and season with ground black pepper.

2 Bring to the boil, then reduce the heat, cover the casserole and simmer for 20 minutes or until the chicken is tender.

3 Lift the chicken out of the casserole and put to one side. Bubble the sauce for 5 minutes or until thickened, then add the olives and capers, stir well and cook for a further 2–3 minutes.

4 Put the chickenback into the sauce. Serve with brown rice and broad beans or peas.

Serves 4

Chicken Tagine

Slow Cooker Recipe

Hands-on time: 10 minutes
Cooking time: 20 minutes in the pan, then 4–5 hours on Low

2 tbsp olive oil

4 chicken thighs

1 onion, chopped

2 tsp ground cinnamon

2 tbsp runny honey

150g (5oz) dried apricots

75g (3oz) blanched almonds

125ml (4fl oz) hot chicken stock

salt and freshly ground black pepper

flaked almonds to garnish

couscous to serve

1 Heat 1 tbsp of the oil in a large pan over a medium heat. Add the chicken and fry for 5 minutes or until brown, then transfer to the slow cooker.

2 Heat the remaining oil in the pan, add the onion and fry for 10 minutes or until softened.

3 Add the cinnamon, honey, apricots, almonds and hot stock to the onion and season well. Bring to the boil, then transfer to the slow cooker, cover and cook on Low for 4–5 hours until the chicken is tender and cooked through.

4 Garnish with flaked almonds and serve hot with couscous.

WITHOUT A SLOW COOKER

Cook the tagine in a large flameproof casserole. Complete step 1 and transfer the chicken to a plate. Complete step 2, then put the chickenback into the casserole and add the ingredients as described at the start of step 3. Cover and bring to the boil, then reduce the heat and simmer for 45 minutes or until the chicken is falling off the bone. Garnish and serve as described in step 4.

Serves 4

Spicy Pork and Bean Stew

Slow Cooker Recipe

🍴 **Hands-on time:** 15 minutes
Cooking time: about 25 minutes in the pan, then 3–4 hours on Low

3 tbsp olive oil

400g (14oz) pork tenderloin, cubed

1 red onion, sliced

2 leeks, trimmed and cut into chunks

2 celery sticks, cut into chunks

½ tbsp harissa paste

1 tbsp tomato purée

400g can cherry tomatoes

150ml (¼ pint) hot vegetable or
  chicken stock

400g can cannellini beans, drained
  and rinsed

1 marinated red pepper, sliced

salt and freshly ground black pepper

freshly chopped flat-leafed parsley
  to garnish

Greek-style yogurt, lemon wedges and
  bread to serve

1 Heat 2 tbsp of the oil in a large pan. Add the pork and fry in batches until golden. Transfer to the slow cooker.

2 Heat the remaining oil in the pan, add the onion and fry for 5–10 minutes until softened. Add the leeks and celery and cook for 5 minutes. Add the harissa and tomato purée and cook for 1–2 minutes, stirring all the time. Add the tomatoes and hot stock and season well. Bring to the boil, then pour into the slow cooker, cover and cook on Low for 3–4 hours.

3 Stir in the beans and red pepper and leave to stand for 5 minutes to warm through. Garnish with parsley and serve with a dollop of Greek-style yogurt, a grinding of black pepper, lemon wedges for squeezing over the stew, and chunks of crusty baguette or wholegrain bread.

An easy way to get a brand new dish is to use the same quantity of lean lamb, such as leg, trimmed of excess fat and cut into cubes, instead of the pork .

Serves 4

One-pot Gammon Stew

Hands-on time: 15 minutes
Cooking time: 1 hour 10 minutes

1 tbsp olive oil

1.1kg (2½lb) smoked gammon joint

8 shallots, chopped into chunks

3 carrots, chopped into chunks

3 celery sticks, chopped into chunks

4 large Desiree potatoes, unpeeled

450ml (¾ pint) apple juice

450ml (¾ pint) hot vegetable stock

½ small Savoy cabbage

25g (1oz) butter

1 Preheat the oven to 190°C (170°C fan oven) mark 5. Heat the oil in a large flameproof casserole, add the gammon and cook for 5 minutes or until brown all over. Remove from the pan.

2 Add the shallots, carrots and celery to the pan and fry for 3–4 minutes until starting to soften.

3 Put the gammon back into the pan. Chop the potatoes into quarters and add to the pan with the apple juice and hot stock. Cover and bring to the boil, then transfer to the oven and cook for 50 minutes or until the meat is cooked through and the vegetables are tender.

4 Take out of the oven and put the dish back on the hob over a low heat. Shred the cabbage and stir into the pan. Simmer for 2–3 minutes, then stir in the butter and serve.

Mexican Chilli con Carne

Slow Cooker Recipe

Hands-on time: 10 minutes
Cooking time: 25 minutes in pan, then 4–5 hours on Low

2 tbsp olive oil

450g (1lb) minced beef

1 large onion, finely chopped

½–1 tsp hot chilli powder

½–1 tsp ground cumin

3 tbsp tomato purée

150ml (¼ pint) hot beef stock

400g can chopped tomatoes with garlic
(see Save Effort)

25g (1oz) plain chocolate

400g can red kidney beans, drained
and rinsed

2 × 20g packs fresh coriander, chopped

salt and freshly ground black pepper

guacamole, salsa, soured cream, grated
cheese, tortilla chips and pickled
chillies to serve

1 Heat 1 tbsp of the oil in a large pan
and fry the beef for 10 minutes or until
well browned, stirring to break up
any lumps. Remove from the pan
with a slotted spoon and transfer to
the slow cooker.

2 Add the remaining oil to the pan, then
fry the onion, stirring, for 10 minutes
or until soft and golden.

3 Add the spices and fry for 1 minute,
then add the tomato purée, hot stock
and the tomatoes. Bring to the boil,
then stir into the mince in the slow
cooker. Cover and cook on Low for
4–5 hours.

4 Stir in the chocolate, kidney beans
and coriander and season with salt
and ground black pepper, then leave
to stand for 10 minutes. Serve with
guacamole, salsa, soured cream,
grated cheese, tortilla chips and
pickled chillies.

Complete step 1 but transfer the beef to a plate. Complete step 2. At the end of step 3, leave the mixture in the pan, put the beef back into the pan and simmer, uncovered, for 35-40 minutes until thickened. Stir in the ingredients as described in step 4 and simmer for 5 minutes. Serve as described in step 5.

SAVE EFFORT

Instead of a can of tomatoes with garlic, use a can of chopped tomatoes and 1 crushed garlic clove. Adding a little dark chocolate to chilli con carne brings out the flavours of this tasty dish.

Serves 4

Top 5 Tips for Gluten-free Cooks

Preventing cross-contamination

- ❑ Have separate areas for food preparation or make sure you thoroughly clean the area if you have used gluten containing food beforehand
- ❑ Store wheat, barley or rye flour and oats away from gluten-free flours
- ❑ Use separate utensils for gluten-free cooking, e.g. chopping board, whisk, knives, sieve, rolling pin, pastry brush
- ❑ Use separate tubs of margarine or butter or always put a clean knife into the tub
- ❑ Use a separate toaster for gluten-free bread

Making bread

Bread made without gluten will have a different texture from breads made with wheat flour. You can make your own using a gluten-free bread flour mixes, made from a combination of rice and tapioca flour. The dough will be softer and stickier than ordinary bread dough so use a heavy-duty mixer or bread machine for mixing. Gluten-free bread also tends to dry out faster, so store it tightly wrapped or freeze bread or rolls soon after baking. Thaw only the amount you're going to eat immediately

Baking cakes

Cakes made with gluten-free flour can be dense and dry but you can avoid this by:

1 Beating the batter longer than normal – around 3–5 minutes to incorporate extra air. The protein and starch in the flour and eggs will form around the air bubbles.

2 Adding extra baking powder or bicarbonate of soda to the mixture.

3 Substituting sparkling water for some of the liquid to add more air to the batter.

4 Use brown sugar in recipes – it has more moisture than white sugar, produces a softer texture.

Gluten substitutes

Gluten-free flour tends to be heavier and absorb more liquid than wheat flour. For cakes and biscuits, add a gluten substitute to the gluten-free flour mixture. For each 125g (4oz) of gluten-free flour mix, add 1 tsp of gluten substitute. Here are three very good substitutes for gluten, which are available in the 'Free Form' section of supermarkets and health shops.

❑ Xanthum Gum
❑ Guar Gum
❑ Gluten-free baking powder

Making pastry

When making pastry with gluten-free flour, cream the flour and butter together rather than using the traditional method of rubbing the fat into the flour. Using this special creaming method helps reduce cracking of the pastry. Other essential tips include making sure you use butter and also to knead the pastry for a full 2 minutes before rolling out.

Curried Lamb with Lentils

Hands-on time: 15 minutes, plus marinating
Cooking time: 20 minutes in pan, then 5–6 hours on Low

500g (1lb 2oz) lean stewing lamb on the bone, cut into 8 pieces (ask your butcher to do this), trimmed of fat

1 tsp ground cumin

1 tsp ground turmeric

2 garlic cloves, crushed

1 medium fresh red chilli, seeded and chopped (see Safety Tip, page 71)

2.5cm (1in) piece fresh root ginger, peeled and grated

2 tbsp vegetable oil

1 onion, chopped

400g can chopped tomatoes

2 tbsp vinegar

175g (6oz) red lentils, rinsed

salt and freshly ground black pepper

fresh coriander sprigs to garnish

rocket salad to serve

1 Put the lamb into a shallow sealable container and add the spices, garlic, chilli, ginger, salt and ground black pepper. Stir well to mix, then cover and chill for at least 30 minutes.

2 Heat the oil in a large pan. Add the onion and cook over a low heat for 5 minutes. Add the lamb and cook for 10 minutes, turning regularly, or until the meat is evenly browned.

3 Add the tomatoes, vinegar, lentils and 225ml (8fl oz) boiling water and bring to the boil. Season well. Transfer to the slow cooker, cover and cook on Low for 5–6 hours until the lamb is tender.

4 Serve hot, garnished with coriander sprigs, with a rocket salad.

Complete the recipe to the end of step 3, then leave the mixture in the pan. Bring to the boil, then reduce the heat, cover the pan and simmer for 1 hour. Remove the lid and cook for 30 minutes, stirring occasionally, or until the sauce is thick and the lamb is tender. Serve as described in step 4.

Serves 4

Cakes and Bakes

Gluten-free Baking

Gluten-free baking is really quite straightforward if you follow the recipe exactly and have the right ingredients. You can adapt your favourite recipes by substituting a gluten-free flour for wheat flour. Safe grains for baking include brown rice flour, white rice flour, tapioca flour and millet. Starches for baking include potato starch, cornflour, arrowroot and tapioca starch. Soybean and chickpea flour, as well as ground almonds are high protein non-grain options.

4 Gluten-free flours

White Rice Flour

This is an excellent basic flour for gluten-free baking. It is milled from polished white rice. Because it has a bland flavour, it is perfect for baking, as it doesn't impart any flavours. It works well mixed with other flours.

Brown Rice Flour

This flour comes from unpolished brown rice. It has more food value because it contains bran. Use it in breads, muffins and biscuits.

Soya Flour

This nutty tasting flour has a high protein and fat content. It is best when used in combination with other flours and for baking brownies or any baked goods with nuts or fruit.

Tapioca Flour

This is a light, white, very smooth flour that comes from the cassava root. It makes baked goods impart a nice chewy taste. Use it in recipes where a chewy texture would be desirable. It would work nicely in bread recipes such as white bread or French bread. It is also easily combined with cornflour and soya flour.

Gluten-free flour mix for cakes and biscuits

700g (1½lb) fine white rice flour
200g (7oz) potato flour
100g (3½oz) tapioca flour

Gluten-free flour mix for bread

400g (14oz) soya flour
200g (7oz) tapioca flour
400g (14oz) potato flour
300g (11oz) cornflour

Gluten-free flour mixes

You can buy gluten-free flour mixes at most supermarkets; self-raising flour as well as plain flour. They usually contain a mix of gluten-free flours like soya and rice flours and some starches like potato starch or tapioca starch. They can be used in the same way that you would use normal flour to bake bread, biscuits, scones, batters, pastries, sauces and Yorkshire pudding.

Fruity Teacake

Hands-on time: 15 minutes, plus soaking
Cooking time: about 1 hour, plus cooling

150ml (¼ pint) hot black tea, made with
   2 Earl Grey tea bags

200g (7oz) sultanas

75g (3oz) ready-to-eat dried figs, hard
   stalks removed, roughly chopped

75g (3oz) ready-to-eat dried prunes,
   roughly chopped

a little vegetable oil

125g (4oz) dark muscovado sugar

2 medium eggs, beaten

225g (8oz) gluten-free plain flour

2 tsp gluten-free baking powder

2 tsp ground mixed spice

butter to serve (optional)

1 Pour the tea into a bowl and add all
  the dried fruit. Leave to soak for
  30 minutes.

2 Preheat the oven to 190°C (170°C fan
  oven) mark 5. Oil a 900g (2lb) loaf tin
  and base-line with greaseproof paper.

3 Beat the sugar and eggs together in
  a large bowl until pale and slightly
  thickened. Add the flour, baking
  powder, mixed spice and soaked dried
  fruit and tea, then mix together well.
  Spoon the mixture into the prepared
  tin and level the surface.

4 Bake on the middle shelf of the oven
  for 45 minutes–1 hour. Leave to cool in
  the tin.

5 Serve sliced, with a little butter if
  you like.

SAVE TIME

Wrap in clingfilm and store in an
airtight container. It will keep for up
to five days.

Cuts into 12 slices

Figgy Fruit Slice

500g (1lb 2oz) ready-to-eat dried figs, hard stalks removed

50g (2oz) candied orange peel, finely chopped

75g (3oz) hazelnuts, toasted

50g (2oz) shelled pistachio nuts

50g (2oz) plain chocolate, broken into pieces

50g (2oz) ready-to-eat pitted dates

¼ tsp ground cinnamon

a pinch of freshly grated nutmeg

4 tbsp brandy, plus extra to drizzle

rice paper

SAVE TIME

If not serving straight away, wrap in baking parchment and tie up with string. Store in the fridge for up to four weeks, unwrapping and drizzling with 1 tsp brandy every week.

1 Put the figs and candied orange peel into a food processor and whiz for 1 minute to mince the fruit finely. Tip into a large bowl.

2 Put the hazelnuts, pistachio nuts, chocolate and dates in the food processor with the spices and 4 tbsp brandy and pulse to chop roughly. Add to the fig mixture and mix, using your hands.

3 Put a sheet of rice paper on a baking sheet. Spoon the fig mixture evenly on top, then press down with the back of a wet spoon to form an even layer about 2cm (¾in) thick. Put another sheet of rice paper on top and press down well. Chill for 1 hour.

4 Cut the slice into four rectangles to serve.

Serves 4

Macaroons

Hands-on time: 10 minutes
Cooking time: about 15 minutes, plus cooling

2 medium egg whites
125g (4oz) caster sugar
125g (4oz) ground almonds
¼ tsp almond extract
22 blanched almonds

SAVE EFFORT

An easy way to get a brand new dish is to make Coffee Macaroons: replace 15g (½oz) of the ground almonds with espresso powder and mix together before stirring into the egg mixture.

1 Preheat the oven to 180°C (160°C fan oven) mark 4 and line two baking sheets with baking parchment.

2 Put the egg whites into a large grease-free bowl and, using a hand-held electric whisk, beat until they form stiff peaks. Gradually fold in the sugar, then gently stir in the almonds and almond extract.

3 Spoon teaspoonfuls of the mixture on to the baking sheets, spacing them slightly apart and press an almond into each.

4 Bake for 12–15 minutes until just golden and firm to the touch. Leave on the baking sheets for 10 minutes, then transfer to a wire rack and leave to cool completely.

Makes 22

Chocolate Cake

Hands-on time: 25 minutes
Cooking time: about 1 hour, plus cooling

125g (4oz) unsalted butter, softened, plus extra to grease

200g (7oz) light muscovado sugar

2 large eggs, lightly beaten

125g (4oz) plain chocolate, broken into pieces, melted and left to cool slightly

100g (3½oz) natural yogurt

a few drops of vanilla extract

200g (7oz) brown rice flour

½ tsp gluten-free baking powder

1 tsp bicarbonate of soda

For the icing

150g (5oz) plain chocolate, broken into pieces

150ml (¼ pint) double cream

large milk and plain or white chocolate buttons to decorate

1 Preheat the oven to 180°C (160°C fan oven) mark 4. Grease a deep 18cm (7in) square cake tin and line with greaseproof paper.

2 Cream the butter and sugar together until light and fluffy. Gradually beat in the eggs, then the melted chocolate, yogurt and vanilla extract. Sift the rice flour, baking powder and bicarbonate of soda together, then beat into the mixture a little at a time.

3 Pour into the prepared tin and bake for 45 minutes–1 hour until a skewer inserted into the centre comes out clean. Cool in the tin for 10 minutes, then turn out on to a wire rack and leave to cool completely.

4 To make the icing, put the chocolate into a heatproof bowl. Heat the cream to just below boiling point. Pour on to the chocolate and leave for 5 minutes, then beat until the chocolate has melted and the mixture is smooth. Cool until thickened, then, using a palette knife, spread all over the cake.

Decorate the top and sides of the cake with alternate milk and plain or white chocolate buttons to create a polka-dot effect.

SAVE TIME

Store in an airtight container. It will keep for up to three days.

Cuts into 10 slices

Sticky Lemon Polenta Cake

Hands-on time: 15 minutes
Cooking time: about 1 hour, plus cooling

50g (2oz) unsalted butter, softened, plus
    extra to grease

3 lemons

250g (9oz) golden caster sugar

250g (9oz) instant polenta

1 tsp gluten-free baking powder

2 large eggs

50ml (2fl oz) semi-skimmed milk

2 tbsp natural yogurt

2 tbsp poppy seeds

1 Preheat the oven to 180°C (160°C fan oven) mark 4. Lightly grease a 900g (2lb) loaf tin and base-line with greaseproof paper.

2 Grate the zest of 1 lemon and put into a food processor with the butter, 200g (7oz) of the sugar, the polenta, baking powder, eggs, milk, yogurt and poppy seeds, then whiz until smooth. Spoon the mixture into the prepared tin and level the surface. Bake for 55 minutes–1 hour until a skewer inserted into the centre comes out clean. Leave to cool in the tin for 10 minutes.

3 Next, make a syrup. Squeeze the juice from the zested lemon plus 1 more lemon. Thinly slice the third lemon. Put the lemon juice into a pan with the remaining sugar and 150ml (¼ pint) water. Add the lemon slices, bring to the boil and bubble for about 10 minutes until syrupy. Take the pan off the heat and leave to cool for 5 minutes. Remove the lemon slices from the syrup and put to one side.

4 Slide a knife around the edge of the cake and turn out on to a serving plate. Pierce the cake in several places with a skewer, spoon the syrup over it and decorate with the lemon slices.

SAVE TIME

Wrap in clingfilm and store in an airtight container. It will keep for up to three days.

Cuts into 12 slices

Lemon Drizzle Loaf

Hands-on time: 20 minutes
Cooking time: about 50 minutes, plus cooling

175g (6oz) unsalted butter, softened, plus extra to grease

175g (6oz) caster sugar

4 medium eggs, lightly beaten

3 lemons

125g (4oz) gluten-free self-raising flour

50g (2oz) ground almonds

75g (3oz) sugar cubes

1 Preheat the oven to 180°C (160°C fan oven) mark 4. Grease a 900g (2lb) loaf tin and line with baking parchment.

2 Put the butter and caster sugar into a large bowl and beat together with a hand-held electric whisk until pale and fluffy – about 5 minutes. Gradually beat in the eggs, followed by the finely grated zest of 2 of the lemons and the juice of ½ lemon.

3 Fold the flour and ground almonds into the butter mixture, then spoon into the prepared tin and bake for 40–50 minutes until a skewer inserted into the centre comes out clean. Cool in the tin for 10 minutes, then turn out on to a wire rack and leave to cool until just warm.

4 Meanwhile, put the sugar cubes into a small bowl with the juice of 1½ lemons and the pared zest of 1 lemon (you should have 1 un-juiced lemon left over). Soak for 5 minutes, then use the back of a spoon to roughly crush the cubes. Spoon over the warm cake and leave to cool completely before serving in slices.

SAVE EFFORT

Ground almonds help make this cake extra soft, but you can replace them with an equal amount of gluten-free flour to make it free from nuts too.

Pistachio and Polenta Cupcakes

Hands-on time: 25 minutes
Cooking time: 25 minutes, plus cooling

150g (5oz) shelled pistachio nuts

175g (6oz) unsalted butter, softened

175g (6oz) caster sugar

3 medium eggs

200g (7oz) fine polenta

½ tsp gluten-free baking powder

150g (5oz) ground almonds

grated zest of 2 lemons

2 tbsp milk

For the icing

75g (3oz) unsalted butter, softened

300g (11oz) icing sugar, sifted

juice of 2 lemons

1 Preheat the oven to 180°C (160°C fan oven) mark 4. Line a 12-hole muffin tin with paper muffin cases.

2 Whiz the pistachios in a food processor until really finely chopped.

3 Using a hand-held electric whisk, beat the butter and caster sugar in a bowl, or beat with a wooden spoon, until pale and creamy. Gradually whisk in the eggs until just combined. Using a metal spoon, fold in the polenta, baking powder, ground almonds, lemon zest, milk and 100g (3½oz) of the ground pistachios until combined. Divide the mixture equally between the paper cases.

4 Bake for 25 minutes or until golden and risen. Leave to cool in the tin for 5 minutes, then transfer to a wire rack to cool completely.

5 For the icing, put the butter into a bowl and whisk until fluffy. Gradually whisk in half the icing sugar, then add the lemon juice and the remaining icing sugar, whisking until light and fluffy. Using a small palette knife, spread a little of the buttercream over the top of each cake, then sprinkle with a little of the remaining chopped pistachios.

SAVE TIME

Store in an airtight container. They will keep for three to five days.

Makes 12

Cake Troubleshooting

Use this handy guide to help you find out where and why things might have gone wrong with your cake baking.

Dos and don'ts of cake-making

How to make perfect cakes

- ❑ Weigh out all the ingredients carefully before starting the recipe, so that you have everything to hand when you begin to make the cake
- ❑ Always work in metric or imperial – never mix the two measurements
- ❑ Check that you have the correct cake tin for the job. The tin sizes quoted in this book refer to the base measurement of the tin
- ❑ Always line the tin properly where necessary
- ❑ Allow the oven to preheat to the correct temperature

- ❑ Try not to be heavy-handed – when folding in flour, use light strokes so that the air doesn't get knocked out
- ❑ Don't let a cake mixture sit around once you've made it: pop it straight into the cake tin and into the oven, otherwise the raising agents will start to react
- ❑ After it has come out of the oven, leave the cake in the tin to cool for 10 minutes, or according to the recipe, and then turn out on to a wire rack to cool completely
- ❑ Let the tins cool completely before washing them in warm, soapy water with a non-abrasive sponge

The cake sinks in the middle
- ❏ The oven door was opened too soon
- ❏ The cake was under-baked.
- ❏ The ingredients haven't been measured accurately
- ❏ The wrong size cake tin may have been used

The cake has a cracked, domed top
- ❏ The oven temperature was too hot
- ❏ The cake was too near the top of the oven
- ❏ Insufficient liquid was used
- ❏ The baking tin was too small
- ❏ Too much raising agent was used

The cake has a dense texture
- ❏ The mixture curdled when the eggs were being added
- ❏ Too much liquid was used
- ❏ The mixture was over-folded
- ❏ Too little raising agent was used or an ineffective raising agent that was past its 'use-by date' was used

The fruit has sunk to the bottom
- ❏ The mixture was too soft to support the weight of the fruit This is liable to happen if the fruit was too sticky or wet

The cake edges are crunchy
- ❏ The baking tin was over-greased

Banana Cake

Hands-on time: 20 minutes
Cooking time: about 1 hour, plus cooling

125g (4oz) unsalted butter, softened, plus extra to grease

125g (4oz) light muscovado sugar

2 large eggs, lightly beaten

50g (2oz) smooth apple sauce

3 very ripe bananas, about 375g (13oz) peeled weight, mashed

1½ tsp mixed spice

150g (5oz) gluten-free plain flour blend

1 tsp gluten-free baking powder

a pinch of salt

For the icing

75g (3oz) unsalted butter, softened

100g (3½oz) icing sugar, sifted

50g (2oz) light muscovado sugar

½ tbsp milk (optional)

dried banana chips to decorate (optional)

1 Preheat the oven to 180°C (160°C fan oven) mark 4. Grease the base and sides of a 900g (2lb) loaf tin and line with baking parchment.

2 Using a hand-held electric whisk, beat the butter and muscovado sugar in a large bowl until pale and creamy. Gradually whisk in the eggs, then the apple sauce. Stir in the bananas.

3 Sift the spice, flour, baking powder and salt into the bowl, then use a large metal spoon to fold in (the mixture may look a little curdled). Spoon the mixture into the prepared tin and bake for 50 minutes–1 hour until risen and a skewer inserted into centre comes out clean. Cool in the tin for 10 minutes, then turn out on to a wire rack (leave the lining paper on) and leave to cool completely.

4 Peel off the lining paper and put the cake on a serving plate.

5 To make the icing, whisk together the butter and both sugars until smooth. If needed, add a little milk to loosen. Spread over the top of the cooled cake. Decorate with banana chips, if you like. Slice the loaf to serve.

Cuts into 8–10 slices

Coconut Cake

Hands-on time: 20 minutes
Cooking time: about 40 minutes, plus cooling

150g (5oz) dairy-free sunflower spread,
  plus extra to grease

finely grated zest and juice (about 3 tbsp)
  of 1 orange

100ml (3½fl oz) coconut milk

75g (3oz) ground almonds

1 large egg

1 tsp gluten-free baking powder

125g (4oz) caster sugar

125g (4oz) gluten-free plain flour blend

50g (2oz) desiccated coconut, optional

For the icing

40g (1½oz) caster sugar

1 tsp cream of tartar

1 tbsp egg white

a few drops vanilla extract

toasted coconut flakes (optional),
  to decorate

1 Preheat the oven to 180°C (160°C fan oven) mark 4. Grease and line an 18cm (7in) round cake tin with baking parchment.

2 To make the cake, put all the cake ingredients into a food processor and pulse to combine (alternatively, beat by hand in a large bowl). Scrape the mixture into the prepared tin and bake for 35–40 minutes or until golden on top and a skewer inserted into the centre comes out clean. Cool in the tin for 10 minutes, then remove from the tin and cool completely on a wire rack.

3 For the icing, put the sugar and cream of tartar into a small bowl and add 2 tbsp boiling water. Stir to dissolve. Put the egg white into a separate medium bowl and start whisking with hand-held electric beaters. With the motor running, gradually add the sugar mixture. Continue beating until the icing holds stiff peaks – about 5 minutes. Beat in the vanilla.

4 Spread the icing on top of the cooled cake and decorate with coconut flakes, if you like. Serve in slices.

Serves 8

Toasted Hazelnut Meringue Cake

Hands-on time: 10 minutes
Cooking time: 30 minutes, plus cooling

oil to grease

175g (6oz) skinned hazelnuts, toasted

3 large egg whites

175g (6oz) golden caster sugar

250g tub mascarpone

285ml (9½fl oz) double cream

3 tbsp Bailey's Irish Cream liqueur

140g (4½oz) frozen raspberries

340g jar redcurrant jelly

1 Preheat the oven to 190°C (170°C fan oven) mark 5. Lightly oil two 18cm (7in) sandwich tins and base-line with baking parchment. Whiz the hazelnuts in a food processor until finely chopped.

2 Put the egg whites into a large, grease-free bowl and whisk until stiff peaks form. Whisk in the sugar, a spoonful at a time. Using a metal spoon, fold in half the nuts. Divide the mixture equally between the tins and spread evenly.

3 Bake both cakes on the middle shelf of the oven for about 30 minutes, then leave to cool in the tins for 30 minutes.

4 To make the filling, put the mascarpone into a bowl. Beat in the cream and liqueur until smooth. Put the raspberries and redcurrant jelly into a pan and heat gently until the jelly has dissolved. Sieve, then leave to cool.

5 Use a palette knife to loosen the edges of the meringues, then turn out on to a wire rack and peel off the lining paper. Put a large sheet of baking parchment on a board and sit one meringue on top, flat-side down. Spread one-third of the mascarpone mixture over the meringue. Top with the other meringue, then cover the whole cake with the rest of the mascarpone mixture, and drizzle over the raspberry purée. Sprinkle with the remaining hazelnuts. Carefully put the cake on a serving plate and drizzle with more liqueur, if you like.

Cuts into
8 slices

Basic White Bread

Hands-on time: 5 minutes, plus kneading
Cooking time: as per your machine, plus cooling

1 tsp easy-blend dried yeast

350g (12oz) gluten-free bread flour, for bread machines

½ tsp salt

1 tbsp olive oil

1 Put all the ingredients into the bread-maker's bucket with 300ml (½ pint) water, following the order and method specified in the manual.

2 Fit the bucket into the bread-maker and set to the programme and crust recommended for gluten-free breads. Press Start.

3 After baking, remove the bucket from the machine, then turn out the loaf on to a wire rack and leave to cool.

SAVE TIME

To make ahead and freeze, complete the recipe. Once the bread is cold, slice, if you like, for convenience, then pack, seal and freeze. To use, thaw at a cool room temperature.

Makes 1 small loaf — cuts into 8 slices

Something
Sweet

Almond Toffee Meringues

Hands-on time: 35 minutes, plus cooling and chilling
Cooking time: about 25 minutes, plus overnight cooling

oil to grease

25g (1oz) light muscovado sugar

100g (3½oz) egg whites (about
  3 medium eggs)

225g (8oz) caster sugar

25g (1oz) flaked almonds

Marinated Fruit (see right) and lightly
  whipped cream to serve

1 Preheat the grill. Lightly oil a baking
  sheet and sprinkle the muscovado
  sugar over it. Grill for 2–3 minutes
  until the sugar begins to bubble and
  caramelise. Cool for about 15 minutes,
  then break the sugar into a food
  processor and whiz to a coarse powder.

2 Put the egg whites and caster sugar
  into a large clean grease-free bowl
  over a pan of gently simmering water,
  making sure the base of the bowl
  doesn't touch the water. Stir until the
  sugar has dissolved and the egg white
  is warm – about 10 minutes.

3 Preheat the oven to 170°C (150°C fan
  oven) mark 3. Remove the bowl from
  the heat and place on a teatowel.
  Using a hand-held electric whisk, beat
  for 15 minutes or until cold and glossy;
  the egg whites should stand in stiff
  shiny peaks when the whisk is lifted.

4 Cover two baking sheets with non-
  stick baking parchment. Fold half
  the powdered caramelised sugar into
  the meringue mixture. Spoon four
  oval mounds on to the baking sheets,
  leaving plenty of space between each.
  Sprinkle with flaked almonds and the
  remaining powdered sugar. Bake for
  20 minutes, then turn off the heat and
  leave in the oven to dry out overnight.
  Serve with the fruit and cream.

Marinated Fruit

Put 125ml (4fl oz) crème de cassis, the juice of 1 orange and 2 tbsp redcurrant jelly in a small pan. Heat gently to melt, then bubble for 2–3 minutes until syrupy. Pour into a large bowl to cool. Add 200g (7oz) raspberries and 4 halved, stoned and sliced nectarines and stir gently.

Cover and chill in the fridge. The flavour of the marinated fruit will be even better if you chill it overnight. (If the syrup thickens during chilling, stir in 1–2 tbsp orange juice.)

Serves 4

Peach Brûlée

Hands-on time: 10 minutes
Cooking time: about 10 minutes

4 ripe peaches, halved and stoned
8 tsp soft cream cheese
8 tsp golden caster sugar

1 Preheat the grill until very hot. Fill
   each stone cavity in the fruit with
   2 tsp cream cheese, then sprinkle each
   one with 2 tsp sugar.
2 Put the fruit halves on a grill pan and
   cook under the very hot grill until the
   sugar has browned and caramelised
   to create a brûlée crust. Serve warm.

SAVE EFFORT

An easy way to get a brand new dish
is to use nectarines instead
of peaches.

Serves 4

Fruity Rice Pudding

Slow Cooker Recipe

Hands-on time: 10 minutes
Cooking time: 2–3 hours on Low, plus cooling and chilling (optional)

125g (4oz) short-grain pudding rice
1.1 litres (2 pints) full-fat milk
1 tsp vanilla extract
3–4 tbsp caster sugar
200ml (7fl oz) whipping cream
6 tbsp wild lingonberry sauce

1 Put the rice into the slow cooker with the milk, vanilla extract and sugar. Cover and cook on Low for 2–3 hours. You can enjoy the pudding hot now or leave to cool and continue the recipe.
2 Lightly whip the cream and fold through the pudding. Chill for 1 hour.
3 Divide the rice mixture among six glass dishes and top each with 1 tbsp lingonberry sauce.

WITHOUT A SLOW COOKER

Put the rice into a pan with 600ml (1 pint) cold water. Bring to the boil, then reduce the heat and simmer until the liquid has evaporated. Add the milk, bring to the boil, then reduce the heat and simmer for 45 minutes or until soft and creamy. Leave to cool, then complete steps 2 and 3 to finish the recipe.

SAVE EFFORT

An easy way to get a brand new dish is to serve in tumblers, layering the rice pudding with the fruit sauce – you will need to use double the amount of fruit sauce.

Serves 6

Tropical Granita

Hands-on time: 10 minutes, plus overnight freezing

600ml (1 pint) tropical juice blend

4 tbsp caster sugar

2½ tbsp dark rum (optional)

juice of 1 lime

2 passion fruits

1 In a large bowl, stir together fruit juice, sugar, rum, if you like, and lime juice until the sugar dissolves. Pour into a roasting tin and freeze overnight or until completely solid.

2 Just before serving, halve the passion fruits and scrape the seeds into a small bowl. To serve the granita, scrape the tines of a fork firmly across the surface of the frozen mixture to form small chilled flakes. Spoon the flakes into small glasses, spoon over the passion fruit and serve immediately.

FREEZE AHEAD

Prepare to the end of step 1 up to a week ahead. A day before serving, put a medium freezer-proof serving dish into the freezer to chill for 10 minutes. Take out the frozen granita and scrape into flakes. Working quickly, transfer the flakes to the chilled serving dish and freeze until you're ready to serve. Then spoon the granita into the glasses and decorate.

Mango Gratin with Sabayon

Hands-on time: 10 minutes, plus resting (optional)
Cooking time: 10 minutes

3 large ripe mangoes, peeled, stoned and sliced

5 medium egg yolks

6 tbsp golden caster sugar

300ml (½ pint) champagne or sparkling wine

6 tbsp dark muscovado sugar to sprinkle

crisp sweet biscuits to serve

1 Arrange the mangoes in six serving glasses. Whisk the egg yolks and caster sugar in a large heatproof bowl set over a pan of gently simmering water, making sure the base of the bowl doesn't touch the water, until the mixture is thick and falls in soft ribbon shapes. Add the champagne or sparkling wine and continue to whisk until the mixture is thick and foamy again. Take off the heat.

2 Spoon the sabayon over the mangoes, sprinkle with the muscovado sugar, then blow-torch the top to caramelise, or leave for 10 minutes to go fudgey. Serve with biscuits.

Serves 6

Elderflower and Fruit Jellies

TAKE 5

🍴 **Hands-on time:** 15 minutes, plus chilling
Cooking time: 10 minutes, plus cooling

2–3 tbsp elderflower cordial
200g (7oz) caster sugar
4 sheets leaf gelatine
150g (5oz) raspberries
150g (5oz) seedless grapes, halved

1. Put the elderflower cordial into a large pan and add 750ml (1¼ pints) water and the sugar. Heat gently, stirring until the sugar dissolves.
2. Put the gelatine into a bowl, cover with cold water and leave to soak for 5 minutes. Lift out the softened gelatine, squeeze out the excess water, then add to the pan. Stir until dissolved, then strain into a large jug.
3. Divide the raspberries and grapes among six 200ml (7fl oz) glasses. Pour the liquid over the fruit, then cool and chill for at least 4 hours or overnight.

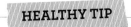

HEALTHY TIP

Gelatine is derived from meat bones, but there are vegetarian alternatives, such as agar agar and gelazone.

Serves 6

Perfect Sorbet

Sorbets have a fine, smooth texture and are most frequently fruit-flavoured. Fruits vary in sweetness, so taste the mixture before freezing. Remove the sorbet from the freezer 20 minutes before serving.

Simple orange sorbet

To serve six, you will need the zest of 3 oranges and the juice of 6 oranges, about 600ml (1 pint), 200g (7oz) granulated sugar, 1 tbsp orange flower water, 1 medium egg white.

1. Put the orange zest and sugar in a pan with 300ml (½ pint) water. Bring slowly to the boil, stirring. Simmer for 5 minutes, leave to cool for 2 minutes, then strain and cool completely.

2. Strain the orange juice into the syrup and add the orange flower water. Chill for 30 minutes.

3. Using an ice-cream maker, follow the manufacturer's instructions but remove the sorbet halfway through.

4. Whisk the egg white, add to the bowl, and continue churning until the sorbet is firm enough to scoop.

2

Granitas

Granita is an Italian water ice with larger crystals than a sorbet. It isn't churned but is broken up with a fork, which makes it more like a frozen fruit slush. Quick to melt, it must be served and eaten quickly and makes a wonderful refresher in summer. Fruit-flavoured, granitas are frequently also popularly flavoured with coffee.

Making by hand

1 Pour the mixture into a shallow container, cover and freeze for about 3 hours, until partially frozen to a slushy consistency. Beat the sorbet with a whisk or fork until smooth.

2 Whisk the egg white and fold into the mixture, then return to the freezer and freeze until firm enough to scoop, 2–4 hours.

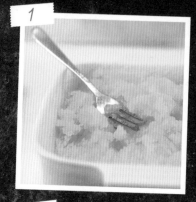

Orange Sorbet

Hands-on time: 20 minutes, plus chilling and freezing
Cooking time: 10 minutes

grated zest of 3 oranges and juice of 6
   oranges – you'll need around 600ml
   (1 pint)

200g (7oz) golden granulated sugar

1 tbsp orange flower water

1 medium egg white

Medjool dates, sliced, and 1 orange, cut
   into segments, to decorate

SAVE TIME

If you're using an ice-cream maker,
add the whisked egg white halfway
through churning, which will give the
sorbet a creamier texture.

1 Pour 300ml (½ pint) water into a
   large pan, add the orange zest and
   sugar and bring slowly to the boil. Stir
   occasionally with a wooden spoon
   to dissolve the sugar. Simmer for
   5 minutes. Leave to cool for 1–2
   minutes, then strain the syrup into
   a clean bowl.

2 Strain the orange juice into the cooled
   syrup and stir in the orange flower
   water. Chill for 30 minutes.

3 Pour the mixture into a shallow 18cm
   (7in) square freezerproof container
   and freeze for 3 hours until slushy.
   Whisk the egg white until stiff, then
   fold into the mixture. Put the sorbet
   back in the freezer and freeze until
   solid – about 2 hours or overnight.

4 Put the sorbet in the fridge for 15–20
   minutes before serving to soften
   slightly. Decorate with Medjool dates
   and orange segments.

Serves 6

Dark Chocolate Soufflés

Hands-on time: 15 minutes
Cooking time: about 20 minutes

50g (2oz) plain chocolate (at least 70% cocoa solids), chopped

2 tbsp cornflour

1 tbsp cocoa powder

1 tsp instant coffee granules

4 tbsp golden caster sugar

150ml (¼ pint) skimmed milk

2 medium eggs, separated, plus 1 egg white

SAVE EFFORT

An easy way to get a brand new dish is to use flavoured dark chocolate for an unusual twist, such as ginger, mint or even chilli.

1 Preheat the oven to 190°C (170°C fan oven) mark 5 and put a baking sheet in to heat up.

2 Put the chocolate into a pan with the cornflour, cocoa powder, coffee, 1 tbsp of the sugar and the milk. Warm gently to melt the chocolate. Increase the heat and stir until the mixture thickens. Allow to cool a little, then stir in the egg yolks. Cover with damp greaseproof paper.

3 Whisk the egg whites in a clean grease-free bowl until soft peaks form. Gradually whisk in the remaining sugar until the mixture is stiff.

4 Stir one-third of egg whites into the chocolate mixture. Fold in the remaining whites and divide among six 150ml (¼ pint) ramekins. Put the ramekins on the baking sheet and bake for 12 minutes until well risen. Serve immediately.

Serves 6

Calorie Gallery

140 cal ♥ 9g protein
4g fat (2g sat) ♥ 4g fibre
24g carb ♥ 0.1g salt
12

108 cal ♥ 3g protein
1g fat (trace sat) ♥ 3g fibre
24g carb ♥ 0.1g salt
14

187 cal ♥ 2g protein
1g fat (0g sat) ♥ 6g fibre
47g carb ♥ 0.1g salt
16

156 cal ♥ 1g protein
trace fat ♥ 2g fibre
40g carb ♥ 0g salt
18

430 cal ♥ 28g protein
20g fat (11g sat) ♥ 0.2g fibre
38g carb ♥ 2.5g salt
32

239 cal ♥ 3g protein
16g fat (6g sat) ♥ 4g fibre
15g carb ♥ 0.4g salt
36

117 cal ♥ 4g protein
6g fat (4g sat) ♥ 4g fibre
13g carb ♥ 0.1g salt
38

110 cal ♥ 9g protein
7g fat (1g sat) ♥ 0g fibre
3g carb ♥ 2.5g salt
50

457 cal ♥ 14g protein
38g fat (18g sat) ♥ 0.9g fibre
5g carb ♥ 1.2g salt
52

138 cal ♥ 10g protein
11g fat (5g sat) ♥ 4g fibre
4g carb ♥ 1.2g salt
54

468 cal ♥ 22g protein
20g fat (3g sat) ♥ 13g fibre
58g carb ♥ 1.4g salt
72

170 cal ♥ 37g protein
2g fat (trace sat) ♥ 0.4g fibre
1g carb ♥ 0.5g salt
74

483 cal ♥ 16g protein
27g fat (4g sat) ♥ 0.1g fibre
40g carb ♥ 1.9g salt
76

348 cal ♥ 33g protein
15g fat (3g sat) ♥ 4g fibre
22g carb ♥ 0.5g salt
78

188 cal ♥ 4g protein
7g fat (1g sat) ♥ 3g fibre
29g carb ♥ 0g salt

20

193 cal ♥ 9g protein
8g fat (1g sat) ♥ 2g fibre
22g carb ♥ 0.3g salt

22

153 cal ♥ 7g protein
14g fat (7g sat) ♥ 0g fibre
1g carb ♥ 0.2g salt

26

263 cal ♥ 18g protein
21g fat (8g sat) ♥ 2g fibre
1g carb ♥ 0.7g salt

28

400 cal ♥ 27g protein
10g fat (5g sat) ♥ 6g fibre
53g carb ♥ 1.5g salt

40

107 cal ♥ 6g protein
4g fat (trace sat) ♥ 2g fibre
9g carb ♥ 1g salt

42

170 cal ♥ 7g protein
14g fat (2g sat) ♥ 3g fibre
7g carb ♥ 0.7g salt

44

503 cal ♥ 62g protein
19g fat (8g sat) ♥ 0.4g fibre
14g carb ♥ 3.8g salt

48

249 cal ♥ 10g protein
9g fat (4g sat) ♥ 1g fibre
31g carb ♥ 0.9g salt

56

197 cal ♥ 14g protein
16g fat (4g sat) ♥ 7g fibre
5g carb ♥ 1.3g salt

58

299 cal ♥ 8g protein
26g fat (5g sat) ♥ 2g fibre
4g carb ♥ 1g salt

60

280 cal ♥ 10g protein
10g fat (1g sat) ♥ 9g fibre
34g carb ♥ 1.3g salt

66

671 cal ♥ 23g protein
28g fat (5g sat) ♥ 3g fibre
70g carb ♥ 0.8g salt

80

568 cal ♥ 34g protein
18g fat (3g sat) ♥ 2g fibre
61g carb ♥ 2.5g salt

82

553 cal ♥ 17g protein
36g fat (12g sat) ♥ 3g fibre
32g carb ♥ 3.4g salt

84

487 cal ♥ 38g protein
21g fat (8g sat) ♥ 12g fibre
45g carb ♥ 1.8g salt

86

564 cal ♥ 43g protein
31g fat (14g sat) ♥ 3g fibre
33g carb ♥ 1.4g salt
88

389 cal ♥ 27g protein
20g fat (7g sat) ♥ 6g fibre
28g carb ♥ 1.2g salt
90

413 cal ♥ 8g protein
17g fat (2g sat) ♥ 5g fibre
57g carb ♥ 0.4g salt
98

399 cal ♥ 20g protein
24g fat (11g sat) ♥ 4g fibre
29g carb ♥ 1.2g salt
100

348 cal ♥ 24g protein
14g fat (3g sat) ♥ 2g fibre
27g carb ♥ 1.5g salt
112

680 cal ♥ 54g protein
30g fat (11g sat) ♥ 6g fibre
41g carb ♥ 6.3g salt
114

116

408 cal ♥ 29g protein
19g fat (7g sat) ♥ 6g fibre
28g carb ♥ 1.1g salt

478 cal ♥ 45g protein
22g fat (7g sat) ♥ 3g fibre
36g carb ♥ 0.3g salt
120

220 cal ♥ 4g protein
7g fat (3g sat) ♥ 0.5g fibre
37g carb ♥ 0.1g salt
134

424 cal ♥ 6g protein
25g fat (13g sat) ♥ 1g fibre
46g carb ♥ 0.6g salt
136

542 cal ♥ 8g protein
33g fat (13g sat) ♥ 2g fibre
56g carb ♥ 0.6g salt

363 cal ♥ 3g protein
18g fat (11g sat) ♥ 0.8g fibre
50g carb ♥ 0.4g salt

138

142

137 cal ♥ 2g protein
6g fat (4g sat) ♥ 2g fibre
21g carb ♥ 0.1g salt
154

323 cal ♥ 7g protein
17g fat (10g sat) ♥ 0.1g fibre
36g carb ♥ 0.2g salt
156

105 cal ♥ 0.5g protein
0g fat ♥ 0.3g fibre
23g carb ♥ 0g salt
158

249 cal ♥ 3g protein
5g fat (1g sat) ♥ 2g fibre
45g carb ♥ 0g salt
160

463 cal ♥ 31g protein
22g fat (6g sat) ♥ 2g fibre
32g carb ♥ 1.8g salt

102

150 cal ♥ 19g protein
3g fat (1g sat) ♥ 2g fibre
10g carb ♥ 0.7g salt

104

327 cal ♥ 27g protein
17g fat (4g sat) ♥ 1g fibre
3g carb ♥ 1.3g salt

108

376 cal ♥ 18g protein
22g fat (4g sat) ♥ 4g fibre
19g carb ♥ 0.5g salt

110

185 cal ♥ 4g protein
1g fat (trace sat) ♥ 2g fibre
42g carb ♥ 0.1g salt

126

577 cal ♥ 10g protein
20g fat (4g sat) ♥ 12g fibre
86g carb ♥ 0.4g salt

128

73 cal ♥ 2g protein
3g fat (trace sat) ♥ 0.5g fibre
10g carb ♥ 0g salt

130

476 cal ♥ 3g protein
28g fat (16g sat) ♥ 0.4g fibre
60g carb ♥ 0.3g salt

132

380 cal ♥ 5g protein
25g fat (9g sat) ♥ 2g fibre
35g carb ♥ 0.6g salt

144

598 cal ♥ 6g protein
38g fat (16g sat) ♥ 2g fibre
57g carb ♥ 0.1g salt

146

130 cal ♥ 2g protein
2g fat (0.2g sat) ♥ 0.7g fibre
27g carb ♥ 0.2g salt

148

without marinated fruit:
294 cal ♥ 4g protein
3g fat (trace sat) ♥ 0.1g fibre
66g carb ♥ 0.2g salt

152

189 cal ♥ 0.5g protein
trace fat ♥ 0.8g fibre
42g carb ♥ 0g salt

162

169 cal ♥ 0.5g protein
trace fat ♥ 0g fibre
44g carb ♥ 0.1g salt

166

134 cal ♥ 4g protein
4g fat (2g sat) ♥ 0.2g fibre
22g carb ♥ 0.1g salt

168

Index

PICTURE CREDITS

Photographers: Neil Barclay (pages 83, 103 and 109); Nicki Dowey (pages 13, 15, 17, 19, 21, 23, 27, 29, 41, 43, 53, 55, 57, 59, 61, 67, 75, 81, 99, 101, 105, 113, 117, 121, 127, 129, 131, 133, 147, 153, 155, 157, 161 and 163); Will Heap (page 45); Gareth Morgans (pages 77, 79, 143 and 145); Craig Robertson (pages 25, 30, 31, 37, 39, 49, 68, 69, 70, 71, 85, 87, 89, 91, 95, 97, 111, 115, 164, 165, 167 and 169); Sam Stowell (page 159); Lucinda Symons (pages 33, 51, 73, 135, 139 and 149), Kate Whitaker (page 137).

Home Economists:
Anna Burges-Lumsden, Joanna Farrow, Emma Jane Frost, Teresa Goldfinch, Alice Hart, Lucy McKelvie, Kim Morphew, Aya Nishimura, Katie Rogers, Bridget Sargeson, Stella Sargeson, Kate Trend and Mari Mererid Williams.

Stylists:
Tamzin Ferdinando, Wei Tang, Sarah Tildesley, Helen Trent and Fanny Ward.

BAKE ME A CAKE
There's always time for cake

EASY PEASY MEALS
Easy meals for every day

LET'S DO BRUNCH
Mouth-watering meals to start your day

CHEAP EATS
Budget-busting ideas that won't break the bank

SALAD DAYS
Oh-so-fresh ideas for fabulous salads

Available online at store.anovabooks.com and from all good bookshops

POSH NOSH
Delicious recipes to impress your guests

PARTY FOOD
Delicious recipes to get the party started

SLOW STOPPERS
Slow-cooked meals packed with flavour

GREAT VEG
Inspired ideas for delicious veggie meals

AL FRESCO EATS
Easy grills, barbecues and picnics

ROAST IT
There's nothing better than a delicious roast

FLASH IN THE PAN
Spice up your noodles and stir-fries

GLUTEN-FREE AND EASY
Oh-so-good-for-you recipes that taste great

LOW FAT LOW CAL
Nice recipes don't need to be naughty